WORD
BIBLICAL
THEMES

General Editor
David A. Hubbard

Old Testament Editor
John D. W. Watts

New Testament Editor
Ralph P. Martin

WORD
BIBLICAL
THEMES

Hosea–Jonah

DOUGLAS STUART

ZONDERVAN ACADEMIC

ZONDERVAN ACADEMIC

Hosea-Jonah
Copyright © 1989 by Word, Incorporated

Requests for information should be addressed to:
Zondervan, *3900 Sparks Dr. SE, Grand Rapids, Michigan 49546*

ISBN 978-0-310-11504-5 (softcover)

Library of Congress Cataloging-in-Publication Data

Stuart, Douglas K.
    Hosea-Jonah: Douglas K. Stuart.
      p. cm.
    Biography: p.
    Includes index.
    ISBN 978-0-849-90784-0
    1. Bible. O.T. Minor Prophets—Criticism, interpretation, etc. I. Title. II. Series.
BS1560.S77 1989
224'.906—dc20   89-33925

Printed in the United States of America

HB 06.21.2021

To my sister Twyla,
student and teacher of the Word

CONTENTS

Contents

FOREWORD

Finding the great themes of the books of the Bible is essential to the study of God's Word and to the preaching and teaching of its truths. These themes and ideas are often like precious gems: they lie beneath the surface and can only be discovered with some difficulty. Commentaries are most useful to this discovery process, but they are not usually designed to help the reader to trace important subjects systematically within a given book of Scripture.

This series, Word Biblical Themes, addresses this need by bringing together, within a few pages, all of what is contained in a biblical book on the subjects that are thought to be most significant to that book. A companion series to the Word Biblical Commentary, this series distills the theological essence of a book of Scripture as interpreted in the more technical series and serves it up in ways that will enrich the preaching, teaching, worship, and discipleship of God's people.

The prophets are not always easy to read or to understand in modern terms. Douglas Stuart's excellent commentary,

Hosea-Jonah in the Word Biblical Commentary series (vol. 31; hereafter referred to in the text as WBC 31), provided detailed scholarly help in understanding these books. Now he has made these helps even more accessible in brief compass by writing on the dominant themes in these books.

The preacher and the teacher will find insights here, not only into the teaching of the prophets, but also into their relation to the Pentateuch and to the New Testament.

Southern Baptist Theological　　　　　John D. W. Watts
　　Seminary　　　　　　　　　　　　Old Testament Editor
Louisville, Kentucky

1   INTRODUCTION

The first five Minor Prophets

In Latin the word *minor* means "smaller," and that—not their relative importance—is what distinguishes the five prophetical books discussed in this volume from their larger (*major*) counterparts. Hosea, Joel, Amos, Obadiah, and Jonah, like the other seven Minor Prophets, are not grouped together as they are by reason of a strict thematic or chronological rationale. Rather, they occur in an order established partly by chronology, partly by content, and partly by an ordering principle not used in modern Western circles, namely, "catchwords" (vocabulary and/or concepts shared by one book with the one after it).

Hosea

The Book of Hosea, the longest of the Minor Prophets, is a collection of prophecies from a northern Israelite prophet who preached to a heedless nation from the 750s until its

1

capture and exile by the Assyrians in the late 720s B.C. Northern Israel had moved, by his day, far from obedience to the covenant that God had revealed to his people though Moses. That history of disregard for God's Law was especially expressed in Israel's turning from orthodox worship to idolatry and polytheism. Baal, the Canaanite weather god, was a more attractive deity to worship than Yahweh, since Baal's specialty was producing rain. Israel, like all ancient societies, was agriculturally based economically and thus extremely rain conscious. By contrast, Yahweh was seen by Hosea's contemporaries as merely a national god, historically Israel's deliverer, but currently less useful than Baal.

Hosea often portrays Israel's consistent unfaithfulness to the true God metaphorically as "prostitution" (Hebrew *znh*). A prostitute is, after all, about as far away from marriage fidelity as is possible to imagine. The frequent employment of the concept of prostitution has, however, led many people to the incorrect conclusion that chapter 1 of the book describes Hosea's marriage to a prostitute at God's direction. In fact, Hosea is told by God only to get married to an Israelite woman, who, no matter her identity, will surely be tainted by the "prostitution" away from the Lord that taints all of Hosea's fellow citizens (1:2). In the prophetic metaphor of marriage relationships, Israel should be Yahweh's faithful wife. Instead, she has deserted him and needs again to be betrothed to him (2:2–20) after an imposed period of confinement (exile; 3:1–5).

A word Hosea uses almost as much as "prostitution" is "return" (Hebrew *šûb*). It is an Old Testament equivalent for "conversion" and conveys often in Hosea the theme of returning to God as Israel's only hope. Return to God and the blessings of his covenant will characterize the new age after Israel's inevitable destruction and exile as a nation—but return to him at any stage by any group, small or large, would also be the people's only avenue of salvation.

The Book of Hosea intersperses prophecies of doom (woe), i.e., Israel's near-term expectation, with prophecies of glorious hope (weal), Israel's long-term certain culmination. Some prophetical books are organized this way (e.g., Isaiah), while others have their passages of woe at the beginning and their passages of weal at the end (e.g., Amos).

During the more than three decades that Hosea preached God's word to usually unresponsive audiences, Israel's fortunes as a nation on the world scene were deteriorating. With the death of Jeroboam II in 753 B.C., Israel's prosperity and independence began to wane. The resurgent superpower Assyria, under its king, Tiglath-Pileser III, increasingly threatened the entire Palestinian area, and by 722 B.C. one of his successors, Sargon II, had captured Samaria and annexed the entire north of Israel to the Assyrian Empire. A succession of Israelite kings, desperately trying to hold the nation together, turned in every direction for help except in the direction of the Lord. Assassinations and usurpations put one king after another on the throne in Samaria, but, as Hosea steadily proclaimed, there was no hope of avoiding conquest by Assyria. Israel's long record of sin had made it unquestionably guilty of breaking God's covenant, and from God's point of view it was "Not My People" (1:9).

Joel

Joel contains the oracles of God given through a sixth-century Judean prophet, from a time when the Babylonians had begun the final act of destruction of the once-proud nation of Judah. Likening the huge, unstoppable Babylonian armies to a swarm of locusts, Joel called for his people to repent—from the least to the greatest, from the drunk to the priest, from the farmers to the young lovers (1:5-14).

Israel's foes were doing Yahweh's bidding. The Babylonian army was merely a sign of, and in one sense an aspect of, the

Day of the Lord (1:15; 2:1-2, 11, 31; 3:14). This theme, noticeably prominent in Joel and Amos, derives from the ancient Near Eastern concept that a truly great king could win any war he fought in a single day. "Day of the Lord" language is used by the prophets to suggest the dramatic and decisive intervention of the Lord as great universal king against his enemies—either morally decadent Israel proximately (1:15; 2:1-2, 11), or the enemies of God's people in the ultimate future (2:31; 3:14).

In addition to his references to Jerusalem via the word "city" (as in 2:9) or "temple" (as in 1:13) and Judah via "the land" (as in 2:1), Joel speaks directly of Zion seven times, Jerusalem six times, and Judah three times. This may reflect Joel's location and his audience: Joel inside Jerusalem under Babylonian siege, preaching to Judeans packed into the city as their last, indeed, forlorn hope of survival.

Joel is perhaps best known for his prophecy of the outpouring of the Spirit of God (2:28-32) quoted by Peter in his Pentecost sermon (Acts 2). Here is the clearest statement in the Old Testament of the important doctrine of the democratization of the Holy Spirit in the New Covenant. What was a rare and selective experience in Old Testament times—the reception of God's Spirit by an individual—became in the new age inaugurated by the coming of Christ the standard experience of *every* believer. The emphasis should indeed rest on "every," since Joel's words underscore the role of the Spirit in the lives of people of both genders, all ages, and all social classes.

Amos

Amos records the words of a Judean sheep breeder and fig cultivation specialist who was inspired by God to preach for a time (perhaps as little as a few months) in northern Israel, around 760 B.C. He was not a professional prophet, trained as a disciple by a senior prophet as, for example, Elisha had been trained by Elijah and had himself trained a company of disciples (7:14-15; cf. 1 Kgs 19:21; 2 Kgs 6:1-2). Nonetheless, under the inspiration of God's Spirit, Amos became so powerful a voice of denunciation of the North's neglect of the covenant that an official attempt was made to silence him (7:10-13).

Considerable attention is given in the Book of Amos to the matter of economic exploitation. The increasing urbanization and cosmopolitanization of Israel in the eighth century B.C. had created a wealthy leisure class (e.g., 4:1; 6:1-7) whose incomes were dependent on taking resources from the poor by means of unfair business practices, aided by manipulation of the legal system (e.g., 2:6-8; 5:7; 8:5-6). In the face of such clear violation of the Mosaic covenant's requirements of both fairness and compassion toward the poor (e.g., Lev 19:9-18), God could hardly accept the otherwise legitimate sacrifices of his people as if there were nothing separating Israel from God's approval (5:21-24).

Like all the prophets whose words touch upon the subject, Amos recognizes the essential unity of the people of Israel, North and South. The northern ten tribes (Israel) had split from Judah (which also subsumed Simeon) in 931 B.C. after the death of Solomon. The divided nation was a political reality, but there is no rift God cannot heal. Amos includes both Judah and Israel at the culmination of a long list of states slated for divine judgment (chs 1 and 2), pairs Zion and Samaria (6:1), refers to the "entire family" of Israel (3:1), and, especially, looks forward to the reunification of North and South under the new David, whom we know to be Christ. Like all the prophets, Amos also foresees under inspiration that the true people of God in the eschaton will not be limited to a Palestinian nation, but will be enormous in scope, "all the nations that bear my name" (9:12).

Obadiah

Obadiah, the shortest book of the Old Testament, is a single-topic book, an oracle against Edom in the classic style of what are called "oracles against foreign nations." It dates probably from about 586–585 B.C., just after the Babylonians had demolished Jerusalem, captured thousands, and sent large numbers of refugees off into the wilderness. Obadiah's prophecy condemns the Edomites for their role in aiding and abetting the Babylonian cause. Edom had been long jealous of and hostile to Israel even though it traced its ancestry to Esau, the brother of Israel's ancestor Jacob. The Babylonian invasion of 588 B.C. proved serendipitous for the Edomites. The Babylonians swept through Judah, conquering all, increasingly driving the surviving Israelites into Jerusalem and then besieging that well-fortified city for two years until its fall in 586. The countryside was completely undefended and ripe for the picking by Edomites, who simply moved out from their confined ancestral mountains to the southeast of Judah, into the farmlands and villages abandoned by the fleeing Judeans (Obad 13). They also took delight in preventing Judeans from escaping the advancing enemy armies (with whom the Edomites had made an early peace) by capturing those heading southeast and turning them over to the Babylonians (Obad 14).

Obadiah not only predicts disasters of lasting consequence for the Edomites as a result of these scurrilous practices, but also describes the future deliverance of Israel from all its enemies and its subjugation of the promised land in the glorious future (vv 17–21).

Jonah

Jonah, unique among the prophetical books, is an account of events in a prophet's life rather than a compilation of his prophecies. Of course, there are both brief and lengthy biographical passages in other prophetical books, and the accounts of Elijah and Elisha in 1 and 2 Kgs, as well as the biographical material about Moses (the "paradigm" prophet, as it were) and other prophets in the Pentateuch and Historical Books provide parallels to Jonah. Nowhere else do any of the sixteen books routinely classified as prophetical concentrate so much on narrative about a prophet and so little on his words.

Especially interesting in Jonah are the descriptions of his motivations. He tried to flee from a God whose influence he may have thought limited to the territory in which he was worshiped (1:3ff.). He clearly resented the possibility that God might use his preaching to bring the hated Assyrians to repentance (1:1; 3:2). He was eloquently grateful at his own undeserved rescue from drowning (2:1-10) but furious at the sparing of the equally undeserving Ninevites (4:1-3). He learned to love a plant, yet begrudged God's loving people and animals, even if they were far from perfect (4:5-9). Jonah is thus a study in hypocrisy, and thereby a warning against the same values in others of any era—including ourselves.

Jonah lived during the reign of the Israelite king, Jeroboam II (793-753 B.C.; 2 Kgs 14:25) and probably made his preaching visit to Nineveh sometime during the kingship of the weak, threatened Aššur-Dan III (773-756 B.C.). The rapid repentance of the Ninevites (3:5-9) was exactly what Jonah had hoped against, but a sovereign God who loves all nations had other plans, and a reluctant prophet became the messenger for a great message of mercy.

2   HOSEA

Hosea, like all the Old Testament prophets, preached on the basis of a special theological understanding of the relationship of God and his people. This understanding was the Mosaic (Sinai) covenant.

A contract bound Israel and her God. The Hebrew word for it is *berît*, commonly translated "covenant." In the New Testament the term is most frequently rendered by the Greek *diathēkē*, but the concept itself is most frequently expressed via the word *nomos*, usually rendered "law." This is because the covenant is indeed a fully legal arrangement, with the penalties of law imposed upon the individual or group—or entire nation—who breaks it. In most modern nations laws are thought to be the products of a society, and it is "society" who is responsible for enforcing the law (via its courts, police, jails, etc., depending on the type of law involved in any given case). In the world of the Old Testament, however, laws were far more likely to be conceived of as originating from a divine source, and Israel's laws, in fact, did.

God, not society, gave the people of Israel their laws, which together constituted the *berît*, covenant, to which the prophets made such frequent reference. There exists a modern Western tendency to regard laws as restrictions on freedom, stemming in part from the huge number of laws enacted during centuries of legislative activity in most Western nations, and the fact that many laws are only selectively enforced because they are widely regarded as archaic or otherwise unfair. The biblical view of the body of laws contained in the Mosaic covenant, however, is that they constitute a generous gift from God, a divine grace for Israel, who without the covenant would be without God's blessing.

The Old Testament covenant is found in the Pentateuch in two interrelated and highly compatible statements. Its "first-generation" statement at Sinai begins in Exod 19 and carries through Lev 26, with a variety of appendices in the Book of Numbers. The "second-generation" statement is found in the bulk of the Book of Deuteronomy. When we speak of a "first generation" we mean the first generation of Israel, which only came officially to be a people when God made it one, at Mount Sinai, when the mixed ethnic and religious stock called Israel gathered there under the leadership of Moses and accepted one God and one faith and one body of law (cf. Exod 12:38; Judg 1:16). The "second generation" was that of their children, who were the ones who actually entered the promised land in fulfillment of the divine oaths to the patriarchs, gaining by default what their parents, by disobedience, had squandered (Num 14:27–35). Both of these statements of the covenant together, consistent with each other as they are while only partly identical in wording, are what the prophets have in mind when they are inspired to call Israel back to covenant obedience to the Lord.

The Old Testament covenant shares with other second-millennium B.C. Hittite and Mesopotamian covenants an elegantly simple structure, consisting of six parts:

Prologue (identification of the parties to the covenant, etc.)
Preamble (historical background explaining how the parties came to the point where they are now united in a covenant)
Stipulations (the actual requirements, or laws; the largest part of most covenants)
Blessings and Curses (rewards and punishments for faithfulness or unfaithfulness, respectively, to the stipulations)
Witnesses (those who confirm that the covenant is in force)
Document Clause (provisions for storage and reading of the covenant document itself)

These are all represented in a manner easy to identify in the Pentateuch, as described by Mendenhall[1] and others.[2]

Underlying all prophetic preaching is the awareness of this covenant relationship of expected obedience. The prophets portray Israel as a nation not in control of its own destiny and not free to choose its own gods or observe its own standards of law. Israel is a nation bound to Yahweh by the Mosaic covenant, and there can be no question that Yahweh will enforce his covenant against those who violate its terms.

Hosea preached that Israel had treated the Lord's covenant "like it was dirt" (6:7). The Hebrew for this descriptive phrase (ke'ādām) has been translated "like Adam" or "as at [the northern Israelite city] Adam," but its most likely literal meaning is simply "like dirt" (see WBC 31:98-99). This is a way of saying that Israel had "betrayed" its Lord (6:7). Of course, such disloyalty or disobedience had its consequences.

God's Covenant with Israel

For Israel those consequences could only be the curses of the covenant as spelled out in the Pentateuch. Among them was conquest in war, and this is what Hosea's words predict, for example, in 8:1-3: "Because Israel has transgressed my covenant . . . the enemy will pursue him." The passage of which 8:1-3 is the beginning concludes at 8:14 with the awesome divine promise: "I will send fire into his cities and it will consume his fortresses." Conquerors typically burned their foes' cities in the ancient Near East, and that was what was going to happen to Israel (cf. 2 Kgs 25:9; Amos 1:4, 7, 10; 2:2, 5; etc.).

Israel's only covenant was to be with Yahweh. Therefore, whenever the nation concluded a covenant with another power, whether religious or diplomatic, they violated their covenant with the Lord. Israel's contract with her God was in the form of what we call a "suzerainty covenant," a covenant of unequal parties. Israel was only the "vassal" in this covenant, inferior and dependent, and at the mercy of her generous protector sovereign, the "suzerain," who was, of course, Yahweh. She had no authority to conclude any covenants on her own, and thus when she tried to do so, which was frequently, she incurred the wrath of her God. Hos 10:4 speaks of the nation's many international treaties in the second half of the eighth century B.C., undertaken in an attempt to shore up Israel's increasingly precarious position between the two great powers of that era, Assyria and Egypt. From
• God's point of view, these international covenants (also translatable as "treaties") were the equivalent of "swearing emptily." They were, moreover, evidences of Israel's "deceit and fraud" (12:1) as Israel made trade agreements with Egypt and political agreements with Assyria (12:4) and vice versa (5:13; 7:11; 8:8-10). They trusted in politics, economics and other religions (2:8, 4:12, 13, 17; 8:6; etc.) and thus scorned the One who should have been their only object of trust

The covenant God had given Israel, however, was not

limited to obligations and punishments; it also contained promises of hope (see also below, Blessings and Curses: The Carrot and the Stick). Thus Hos 2:16-23 envisions a day in the distant future from the point of view of the prophet and his contemporaries when there will be a new people of God, faithful to him alone and the beneficiaries of a new covenant that he will make for them and the whole earth (2:18). This is the new covenant that we who are in Christ have accepted as our own, and that will have its complete fulfillment only in the age that is yet to come.

As the heirs of the promises of the covenant (Gal 3:29) we can identify with the Israelites in relation to it—but only to a point. It is the new covenant, not the old, to which we are parties. Some stipulations of the old covenant have been renewed in the new. These are essentially the Ten Commandments and the two great commandments (loving God and neighbor), all of which originate in the Old Testament (Covenant) and are reiterated in one form or another in the New Testament (Covenant). We are not obligated, however, to obey the Old Testament ritual laws or Israelite civil laws, etc. The same generous God who gave to his people the first law has now given the law of Christ and has both met and exceeded the demands of the first law by the work of his son.

The attractions of idolatry

Throughout Israel's history her loyalty to the Lord was fragile. The Old Testament abounds with references to the nation's practice of idolatry, a habit that automatically violated the first and second of the Ten Commandments (Exod 20:3-6) and thus incurred the judgments associated with violation of the divine covenant.

Hosea often refers to idols and to the whole system of idolatry. In 4:17, Ephraim, an alternate name for (northern) Israel, is described as "in league with idols." In 5:1, the nation is said to have "decided to follow a blah," a scathing attack on the worthlessness of idols (cf. Jonah 2:8, where idols are called, literally, "worthless nothings"). Of course, idolatry had no sanction from God. Israel was on its own, in rebellion, when "with their silver and gold they made idols for themselves." In the coming exile, which Hosea predicts repeatedly and which occurred in 722 B.C., the Israelites would be deprived of things they had come to depend on, including their idols: "for a long time the Israelites will remain without king, without official, without sacrifice, without pillar, without ephod or teraphim" (Hos 3:4).

Israel's attraction to idolatry had manifested itself early in the nation's experience. Accustomed to making idols in Egypt, the people returned to their habit even while Moses was on Mount Sinai receiving formal instructions against the practice (Exod 32). The golden bull idols destroyed at that time were later reproduced by Jeroboam I, the first king of northern Israel (1 Kgs 12:28–33). They were worshiped steadily thereafter, including by Hosea's contemporaries: "At the bull of Beth-Awen the inhabitants of Samaria tremble" (Hos 10:5; Beth-Awen was a satirical name, meaning "House of Nothing," for Bethel, which meant "House of God"). In 13:2, Hosea mocks the fact that in idolatrous worship, "human beings kiss bulls!"

Israel's tendency toward idolatry had also surfaced in the wilderness era, emerging full-blown just before the people were to cross into the promised land. Num 25 records the incident at Baal-Peor, where the people of Israel seemed only too eager to prepare for yielding to the temptations of the land of Canaan by indulging their interest in idolatry and the ritual prostitution associated with it (see below). Hos 9:10 recalls this degeneration into idol worship: "But they came to Baal-Peor, consecrated themselves to 'Shame' and became detestable like their lover."

With idolatry came its superstitions and primitive divination beliefs, including rhabdomancy (the practice of trying to receive divine instruction by seeing which way a stick fell). As well as we can reconstruct this practice from parallels elsewhere in the ancient Near East, a stick or staff was held upright with its lower end resting on the ground in the middle of a circle drawn in the dirt. The circle was divided into sections labeled for the various options one was considering. The stick was dropped, and the option it fell across was considered the option advised by the god(s). Hosea's inspired words protest this outrageously foolish procedure: "He consults his wood! His staff advises him!" (Hos 4:12).

We must remember, however, that idolatry did not seem foolish to ancient people (as it does not seem foolish to the hundreds of millions who worship idols today). As it was observed in Israel in Hosea's day, idolatry had a number of characteristics that made it a most attractive alternative to the revealed religion of the Mosaic covenant. These characteristics may be summarized as follows:

1. *Idolatry claimed to offer results that were guaranteed.* An idol was considered to capture some of the essence of the god or goddess it was designed to represent. If one was in the presence of an idol, one was guaranteed to be in the very presence of the god for which the idol stood. Offerings placed in front of idols had to be accepted (what could the lifeless idol do—shove the stuff away?). Thus the gods had to accept their suppliants' offerings and were automatically obligated to respond by blessing them.

2. *Idolatry indulged the selfish interests of people.* Idolatry was not merely a means of worship using statues. It was an entire system of life, which at its core was thoroughly materialistic. A quid pro quo logic underlay the system. Idols were supposed to give to you if you gave to them. The more you sacrificed, the more they were required to bless

The Attractions of Idolatry

your crops and your herds. A really religious person could become a really wealthy person. Idolatry, in short, was an early version of the modern health-and-wealth gospel (cf. Hos 4:7).

3. *Idolatry was easy.* It allowed ritual without ethics. In other words, frequency and generosity of worship were the sole demands on an idolatrous believer. No covenant bound the believer to live a generous, faithful, upright life, doing acts of love for his or her neighbor and for God. One could be selfish, even viciously oppressive of others, and still be right with the gods as long as one sacrificed frequently and substantially.

4. *Idolatry was convenient.* Hosea describes the Israelites' worship in this way:

> On the mountain tops they make sacrifices;
> On the hills they burn offerings
> Under oak and poplar
> And under terebinth, for their shade is nice. (4:13)

This echoes the statement in Deut 12:2 that pagan worship was conducted "on the hills and under every spreading tree," a phrase repeated often by the prophets. God's revealed Law insisted that his people worship at one place, together, on occasions of his designation (Deut 12:4–32; Exod 23; Lev 23). Idolatrous worship of the kind the Israelites quickly adopted upon entering the promised land required no such inconvenience. People would worship any day of the week, at any place. Pagan shrines dotted the landscape. A bit of a hill, an altar, and some shade to make the process comfortable was all that was needed. By contrast, the orthodox Israelites had to make the long trek to the sole central sanctuary (the temple at Jerusalem in Hosea's day) from wherever they lived, three times yearly.

5. *Idolatry was normal.* It was the standard means of worship, without exception, in the ancient world. Orthodox Israelites were indeed odd by the standards of any nation or group, including their fellow citizens who had abandoned the Lord's covenant. Idolatry was the settled, experienced Canaanite way—it was what had worked for millennia before the Israelites arrived in Canaan. The locals ought to know what was best for agriculture, shouldn't they? They ought to know what worked to make a family wealthy in that particular part of the world, shouldn't they? What about the superpowers (Egypt, Assyria) and the economically successful neighboring states (Tyre, etc.)? Weren't they idolatrous? Hadn't it worked for them? Why practice religion without idols? Why do something completely illogical in the opinion of everyone but a few oddball Yahwistic prophets? Why do something so silly as to worship an unseen god?

6. *Idolatry seemed logical.* It made sense in a society that saw houses or ships built by groups of individuals with various specialties, and saw various types of farmers produce various types of crops and animals, that there must also be a multiplicity of gods. Rather than a single general practitioner (Yahweh), why not a number of gods and goddesses, every one a specialist in his or her own right? Idolatry, in other words, always involved polytheism and syncretism (the tendency to accept different beliefs as valid). This always seemed more appropriate to the majority of the people than putting all of one's eggs in a single religious basket. To idolaters, Yahweh hadn't ceased to exist. He was merely assigned the limited, historically bound role of national deliverer. The idea that he was the only God had been long abandoned.

7. *Idolatry was pleasing to the senses.* It allowed for the painting and sculpturing of images of all sorts (cf. Ezek 8:9ff.) which appealed to peoples' artistic appreciation. It required

bowing down to and kissing idols as one brought one's sacrifices to them (1 Kgs 19:18), thus indulging the natural human tendency to substitute sensory ritual for real obedience (Hos 8:11-13; cf. Amos 5:21-24).

8. *Idolatry was indulgent.* Most ancient people ate meat only as an act of worship and would not have thought of eating meat apart from religious ceremonies. Cooking meat and sharing it with an idol (in reality with the idol's priests) was basic to worship. Orthodox Israelites were allowed to eat meat any time they wished (Deut 12:15, 21). To others this seemed like wasting a perfectly good chance to kill two birds with one stone. Moreover, frequent and large-portioned worship meals accompanied by heavy drinking, out of the question for those faithful to the covenant, were quite acceptable in the idolatrous cults (cf. Amos 2:8).

9. *Idolatry was erotic.* Sex was a regular part of the process. When men brought their sacrifices to the idolatrous shrines, they could—with religious approval!—have ritual sex with the prostitutes there. Such sex was supposed to stimulate the powers of nature to be fertile. Ancients tended to believe that all creation was actually procreation, based on their own limited observation that significant new things (animals, people, and even plants "born" from seeds) came into being by birth. Since idolatry was a system set up to help make people more prosperous, and since in the ancient world all societies were agrarian in economy, to stimulate nature's fertility by having sex with a prostitute seemed a desirable way to worship. Naturally, it was highly self-indulgent. As might be expected, sexual preferences were accommodated. Heterosexuals had sex with women; homosexuals with men (cf. Amos 2:7; 2 Kgs 23:7).

For such systemic violation of God's Law, Israel had to be punished, and much of the Book of Hosea is devoted to predicting and justifying that punishment. Hosea, however, looked beyond Israel's idolatrous past and present to their eschatological future, when God will have cleansed them from their idolatry. In the very last verse of the book (14:8), God states, predictively, "What will Ephraim have to do any more with idols?" The ultimate answer, thank God, is "Nothing."

Prostitution

Marriage is a strong legal bond in every society. As such it has been used often as a metaphor for other strong legal bonds, such as covenants. Prostitution is, however, in one sense the very opposite of marriage. Marriage puts two people together in a long-term relationship; prostitution puts two people together only in a brief encounter. Marriages are threatened by infidelity; infidelity is automatic to prostitution. Marriage is exclusive; prostitution is completely promiscuous. Marriage requires loyalty; prostitution avoids obligation.

These contrasts with marriage made the concept and vocabulary of prostitution appropriate as a way of speaking about covenant breaking, just as the concept and vocabulary of marriage were appropriate to speaking about covenants themselves. A variety of documents from the ancient Near East contain references to covenant breaking via the metaphor of prostitution. Assyrian and Babylonian international treaty correspondence sometimes refers to kings or nations who had broken a treaty as "prostitutes." In the Old Testament, the Hebrew word for prostitution uses the root *znh* in its various derived nominal and verbal forms. This root appears 111 times from Genesis to Nahum. In the majority of instances, the word is used in a metaphorical sense rather than its literal meaning. This is especially the case in the prophetical books, and most especially in one major prophet and one minor prophet, Ezekiel and Hosea. For these two prophets, prostitution (*znh*) is a key vocabulary word, and the concept is a key means of portraying Israel's unfaithfulness to the covenant she was supposed to keep with God.

In Hosea, *znh* appears fifteen times,[3] and only two of these occurrences have reference to literal prostitution. One occasion is found in 4:10, where Hosea speaks of prostitution both literally and figuratively in the same verse:

> They will eat but not be satisfied;
> they will practice prostitution but not break forth,
> because they have abandoned Yahweh to revere
>   prostitution.

This verse is in the form of a "futility curse," a prediction of unfulfilled expectations as a result of sin. The first use of "prostitution" in the verse is literal. It alludes to the ritual cultic prostitution that was designed to stimulate the powers of nature. Through Hosea, God says that the literal prostitution will not work. Israel will not "break forth," that is, be more productive in population and agriculture. In stating the reason for this, the verse makes it clear that Yahweh would not bless Israel because of their revering (figurative) "prostitution," that is, other gods in their infidelity to his covenant. That is what "abandon Yahweh" means in Hosea as well as elsewhere in the Old Testament—the rejection of exclusive faith in and obedience to Yahweh in favor of other faith and worship. Such other faith and worship could be either instead of or in addition to true orthodoxy. It made little difference. Failure to seek and obey only the Lord was religious prostitution.

In 4:14, *znh* is likewise used both literally and figuratively:

> Shall I not punish your daughters, since they turn to
>   prostitution?
> And your daughters-in-law, since they commit
>   adultery?

Indeed, the men make offerings with the prostitutes,
And sacrifice with the cult prostitutes!
A people that lacks understanding must be ruined
   because it turns to prostitution.

Here the literal practice of pagan worship prostitution is
clearly in focus, probably in each of the first four lines. In
typical synonymous parallelisms (here between "daughters"
and "daughters-in-law" and between "prostitution" [znh]
and "adultery" [n'p] in the first couplet), the first line's terms
("daughters" and "prostitution") are paramount—that is, the
topic of individual adultery is not the focus here. In the final
line of the verse "prostitution" has its metaphorical meaning
once again. What has ruined Israel is its rejection of God,
not a single type of immorality, disgusting as literal prostitution is.

At the very outset of the Book of Hosea, Israel's "prostitution" constitutes the metaphorical theme for the opening
prophecy, the subject of which is God's impending rejection
of Israel. In 1:2, God tells Hosea: "Marry a prostituting
woman and (have) prostituting children; because the land
has gone thoroughly into prostitution, away from Yahweh."
The command makes a hyperbolic, that is, purposely exag-
gerative, point: Israel has so little interest in the Lord ("has
gone thoroughly into prostitution") that any woman Hosea
marries and any children he has will almost surely be tainted
by the religious infidelity in the North. This was not an idle
characterization, since, for example, there was not a single
legitimate place of worship in (northern) Israel. Only the
temple at Jerusalem was legitimate, and in Hosea's day it,
too, was corrupted by the presence of shrines for the worship of pagan gods and goddesses. God's command did not
mean that Hosea could not find a decent wife to marry or
that his children would automatically grow up to be idolaters even if he raised them otherwise. It was a way of stating

the seriousness of the apostasy of Israel during the last days of the reign of Jeroboam II (703-753), when this revelation came to Hosea.

One modern translation, the New International Version (NIV), has misjudged the range of meaning of the root *znh* and has rendered Hos 1:2 as follows: "Go take to yourself an adulterous wife and children of unfaithfulness because the land is guilty of the vilest adultery in departing from the Lord." This translation is misleading because adultery, normally rendered in the Hebrew by the root *n'p*, is quite different from prostitution. It is thus used only rarely in the Old Testament as a metaphor for infidelity to God's covenant. The NIV translators of Hosea, apparently motivated by a desire to avoid suggesting that God would command someone to marry a prostitute, ended up implying that he actually married an adulteress, thus missing the whole point of Hosea's regular use of *znh* in a nonliteral manner. Fortunately, this is an isolated aberration, and in other modern translations the reader can easily discern that "prostitution" is normally a figurative reference to unfaithfulness.

Hos 4:12 characterizes Israel as led astray by a "prostituting spirit" (*rûᵃḥ z'nûnîm*). This is a condemnation of a whole society's way of thinking and one of many examples in the Bible of the pervasiveness of corporate sin. The breadth of this corporate sin can be seen in 4:11 and 4:12 together:

> Wine and fruit of the vine dulls the mind of my
>   people!
> He consults his wood!
> His staff advises him!
>
> For a prostituting spirit has led them astray,
> And they are prostituting themselves away from their
>   God.

Hosea cites two instances of Israel's corporate sin as a synecdoche for its pattern of "prostitution." These two are drug abuse (in this case alcohol abuse) and the silly practice of rhabdomancy. These instances of personal debauchery and religious folly, respectively, are evidence of what sort of a national "spirit" inhabits Israel. In 5:4, Israel's prostituting spirit is more broadly characterized by descriptions of the nation's "deeds," their lack of knowledge (i.e., exclusive faithfulness) of the Lord, and their (selfish) pride.

The final appearance of *znh* in Hosea comes at 9:1:

> For you have prostituted yourself away from your
> God.
> You love the prostitute's fee at every grain threshing
> floor.

This suggests a main motivation for the people's infidelity—materialism. Yahweh was just not seen as a fertility God, specially able to bring the kind of rich harvest that would fill the grain threshing floors with an abundance for the year ahead. What the nation wanted was a lot of everything. They wanted wealth and the ease and pleasure it would bring. They failed to find Yahweh attractive any more (cf. 2:7, 13) because faithfulness to him, with all its required self-denial and generosity toward others, was hardly what would meet their materialistic requirements. Israel should have stayed married to her divine husband. Instead, she chose prostitution—and reaped its rewards.

The reliance of the prophets on the Law

In Old Testament times, laws were understood to be paradigmatic rather than exhaustive, and legal citation was therefore an irrelevant idea. A paradigmatic understanding of law holds that it is not necessary in a law code to spell out every possible situation requiring regulation, nor to identify every possible option for punishment in each of those cases. It is enough that a law code should *suggest* how judges and juries should decide civil and criminal legal cases by giving *examples* of misdeeds and typical punishments, or *examples* of regulations that would apply to typical societal practices.

Modern Western law codes are different. They are of the type that we call exhaustive. Every crime is defined precisely in the law code. If it isn't in the law code, it isn't a crime. Regulations must be spelled out in the code, as well. If they aren't there, they aren't binding on anyone and cannot be enforced. Not surprisingly, in an attempt to be exhaustive, modern Western law codes contain thousands of laws printed on thousands of pages. American federal tax laws alone occupy more than a thousand pages of text, and court decisions and Internal Revenue Service guidelines on the federal tax law occupy thousands more. State and local laws and court interpretations magnify the total bulk of the codes all the more. Even so, some people who commit offenses against society are either never brought to justice or are never punished because of what we popularly call "loopholes" in the law. The people who make the laws simply can't think of everything, and the prosecutors or courts interpreting the laws are reluctant to apply any law to any case it does not precisely fit. In other words, the law codes are not really "exhaustive" even though they are supposed to be. Nevertheless, modern Western nations are committed to the exhaustive law philosophy.

Not so in the world of the Old Testament. All law was paradigmatic, and there were no such things as loopholes. Laws gave a general idea to judges and juries of how they should handle crime or civil regulations, but nobody in the legal systems actually referred verbatim to the law codes in deciding a court case. Legal citation, as such, did not exist. Judges and juries reasoned by general analogy to written or common law in deciding court cases—they did not look a case up, read it, and see if its *wording* applied. Instead they used their own good judgment as to whether its *principle* applied. Hammurabi's Law, from about 1700 B.C. in Babylonia, contains 282 laws, a very large number for its day, but still not even remotely "exhaustive." Accordingly, the thousands of court case records that have survived on clay tablets from cities and towns in Babylonia after Hammurabi's Law was widely distributed never once mention the Law or cite any of its provisions. Legal citation was not a practice of that era.

The prophets do not cite the Law of Moses either. That Law has 613 commandments but is still not cited anywhere in the prophetical books. It is cited frequently in the New Testament, but that is because by Roman times legal citation had developed. In the past, some critics of the Old Testament tried to argue that since the prophets never cited the Mosaic Law, it must not have existed in their day, being a later fabrication. This we now know to be a worthless argument. The lack of legal citation, however, does present us with an important theological challenge: discerning how the prophets do in fact refer to the Law if they do not cite it verbatim. The answer, in short, is that they refer to the Law by *allusion*. They don't directly quote it; they allude to its provisions by making statements that are so similar to the Law or so consistent with it that it is obvious that they have it in mind.

Hos 4:2 is a parade example of prophetic allusion to the Mosaic covenant, specifically to the Ten Commandments: "Cursing, lying, murder, stealing, and adultery break forth in the land, and the idols crowd against one another." In this single sentence, six of the ten commandments are alluded to. The correlation may be summarized as follows:

Cursing (Heb. 'lh):Commandment No. 3 (Exod 20:7; Deut 5:11)

Lying (Heb. *khš*):Commandment No. 9 (Exod 20:16; Deut 5:20)

Murder (Heb. *rṣḥ*):Commandment No. 6 (Exod 20:13; Deut 5:17)

Stealing (Heb. *gnp*):Commandment No. 8 (Exod 20:15; Deut 5:19)

Adultery (Heb. *n'p*):Commandment No. 7 (Exod 20:14; Deut 5:18)

Idols (Heb *dāmîm*):Commandment No. 2 (Exod 20:4–6; Deut 5:8–10)[4]

Hosea does not allude to the Commandments in the order they occur in the Pentateuch, nor by the identical vocabulary words in all cases. He is not citing; he is alluding, in the same way that we speak of "freedom of religion" as guaranteed by the U.S. Constitution even though that phrase does not occur in the Constitution, but is only a summary of what the First Amendment says about religion.

Many of the wording choices in the book reveal a dependency on the Pentateuchal Law, and this dependency can be seen especially in statements that make sense only if one knows in detail the content of the Mosaic covenant. For example, in 7:16, Israel's coming judgment for its long history of disobedience to Yahweh is described as resulting in "mockery on them in the land of Egypt." In 8:13, the people are told that the Lord "will remember their guiltiness, and he will punish their sins. Behold they will return to Egypt." Such statements have often puzzled commentators unaware of the significance of the word "Egypt" in Deuteronomy, or of the prophets' awareness of it. Deut 28:68 states that if Israel breaks the covenant, God will send them back in misery[5] to "Egypt." A literal return to the land from which they escaped is not meant, and the statement is enigmatic unless one recognizes that "Egypt" in the covenant curses is a metonymy for "land of exile." Only with this important vocabulary usage of the covenant already established do Hos 7:16 and 8:13 make sense.

Concentrated in the Mosaic Law mainly in Lev 26 and Deut 28–33 are the various types of curses and blessings that constitute the covenant's sanctions. We will discuss these blessings and curses further in the pages just ahead. What is remarkable about their connection with Hosea is that he, like all other prophets, never mentions a prediction of woe or weal that is not an allusion to one of the types already found in the Law. In 1:5, for example, the prediction of destruction via war echoes such predictions as found in Lev 26:25 and Deut 28:49. In 3:5, the promised return from exile alludes to such promises in Deut 4:30 and 30:4–5. In 5:7, the malediction that "a new people will eat their portions" shows a dependence on such Pentateuchal statements as Deut 28:33, "A people you do not know will eat what your land and labor produce." In 13:15, the description of coming drought reflects such predictions as that of Lev 26:19 or that of Deut 28:22–24. And so on.

A final example of Hosea's use of the books of the Law may be seen in 1:9, where God restates his name identically as revealed in Exod 3:14 but in the negative. The name revealed (or more properly, re-revealed) to Moses in Exod 3 in Hebrew is in the first person, Ahyeh rather than Yahweh. Hos 1:9 makes use of this same name, Ahyeh, in the otherwise incomprehensible sentence "You are not my people and I am not your Ahyeh [i.e., not your Lord]." With the Law in mind, the statement has meaning. Without it, the resulting mistranslated Hebrew ("will not be to you" or the like) is strangely awkward.

Blessings and curses: the carrot and the stick

What do the prophets talk about most? In a general sense it is the relationship of Israel to Yahweh. But, specifically, what topics do they most frequently touch upon? If you put your finger randomly on a page of Old Testament prophecy, what would you have the highest statistical chance of pointing to? The answer is: blessings and curses.

Hosea's era (roughly 760–722 B.C.) was that of the end of (northern) Israel. He preached doom, and the words the Lord had given him soon came true. His most frequent assignment was describing covenant curses, explaining their necessity in light of Israel's history of violating the Mosaic covenant. The doomsaying also demanded a broad look at the overall plan of God. After all, eloquent denunciations of the nation and graphic depictions of its coming destruction rouse questions: Is that all? Is Israel's history coming to a complete end? Has God abandoned the nation he rescued from slavery in Egypt and brought to a land of promise? Thus predictions of immediate, short-range miseries lead to predictions about the ultimate, long-range future. Hosea, like other prophets, provides answers to both sorts of concerns, and these occupy the majority of the book that bears his name. Indeed, one can say that nearly all of the material in the book falls into one of three categories:

1. Evidence that curses are warranted (e.g., 1:2; 2:4–5, 13; 4:1–2, 7–8, 10–14, 17–18; 5:1–5, 10–11, 13; etc.)
2. Predictions of curses about to be fulfilled (e.g., 1:4–5, 6, 9; 2:3, 6, 9–13; 3:4; 4:3, 5–6, 9–10, 19; 5:2, 6–10, 14–15; etc.)
3. Predictions of ultimate blessings, to follow the time of the curses (e.g., 1:10–2:1; 2:14–23; 3:5; 6:1–3; etc.)

The parts of passages that contain evidence that curses are warranted are not self-contained units in themselves but subunits within curse passages. That is, one does not find in Hosea passages that describe covenant-breaking sins concluding without saying what will happen as a result. The result (i.e., a curse or curses) is always specified. Indeed, one way that we know we haven't yet come to the end of a full prophetic judgment oracle is if we haven't yet reached the point of learning the curse(s) that will come as a result of the sin being recounted (e.g., 5:8–7:1; 13:2–16).

The passages that contain predictions of ultimate blessings are often, however, self-contained (e.g., 14:1–8). There is little need to describe what Israel will do to redeem itself from exile and divine rejection, that is, the deeds that will precede its restoration blessings. The reason is, simply, that Israel cannot redeem itself. The blessings of the latter days will not be contingent on a long history of good behavior in the same way that the curses of the immediate future are the result of a long history of bad behavior. Restoration blessings are gifts of God's grace, not rewards for deeds.

Neither evidence of sin, nor predictions of curses, nor predictions of restoration blessings are exhaustive. They are, rather, samples of a fuller picture only partly painted by Hosea's inspired words. One or two instances of sin in a passage (e.g., 9:10, 15 in 9:10–17) suffice to suggest a whole range of covenant violations. The mention of one or two types of curses is enough to suggest the full range of divine judgments (twenty-seven types in all) summarized in the curse portions of the Pentateuch (Lev 26 and Deut 28–32). A single kind of restoration blessing is enough to hint at the broad range (ten types in the Pentateuchal lists in Lev 26 and Deut 4 and 30) of good things ahead for the people of God after their judgment is complete.[6]

The Mosaic covenant predicts two kinds of blessings for Israel, immediate and eschatological, but the prophets, including Hosea, predict only one kind. That is a function of their position in history. Hosea, one of the earliest of the classical or "writing" prophets is nevertheless at the end of a major time span in Israel's history as a nation. The time for the immediate, or original, blessings of the covenant had ended. The original blessings were those God gave to the people, as he had promised through Moses, initially upon their entering the promised land and thereafter until their end as an independent nation. Hosea was not called by God to predict any more of *these* blessings because God's plan was now to decimate and exile his people, not to keep blessing them in the land of promise. The original blessing era was ending. Hosea *was* called to predict the other kind of covenant blessing, however—the eschatological kind. The restoration era, when such blessings would be experienced, had obviously not yet arrived, and the Israelites—those, that is, who were even willing to pay attention to the prophets of Yahweh—needed the hope of restoration blessings as an encouragement during the agony of the punishment days just ahead (or already starting; cf., e.g., Amos 4:6–11).

There are more and longer curse passages and their supporting evidence-of-guilt passages in Hosea than there are restoration blessing passages. That is the usual ratio. Hosea's contemporary audience was entering an era of judgment, and God obviously desired that they should not fail to understand what was happening to them (curse) and why (evidence). It is also the case that the stick is more effective than the carrot in some circumstances. When the stick is immediately present and the carrot is a long way off, the carrot may have some effect, but the stick will have more. Thus all of the prophets say somewhat more about the past and present of their contemporaries than about the future, that is the eschatological restoration. Moreover, the majority of those to whom they preached were the objects of wrath rather than of blessing. It makes sense that we should have more of the one than the other.

Quantity is not quality, of course, and our appreciation of theological themes cannot be based solely on ratios of woe to weal in Hosea or other prophetical books. Hosea sees by God's revelation both the near and the distant. Both help shape behavior. While the nation's fate was already sealed, righteous individuals in the mid-eighth century B.C. were yet able to hope for the eventual blessing that the book describes. They lived in a wicked world, just as we do, and could, by trust in God, escape its ultimate consequences. They could also be reassured both by watching God's harsh word come true in their lifetimes, as well as by promises of things that would come to pass even long after their life on earth was over, just as we should be reassured both by the New Covenant promises of the second coming of Christ and the final judgment, looking toward eternal life. These promises guarantee to us that our obedience to the Lord and our membership in his people are not in vain. We see a cursed world but know that its eventual redemption has been secured. Hosea's audience could relate in the same way to the blessings and curses of the Mosaic covenant.

Corporate and individual sin

Hosea uses the word "people" (Heb. 'am) seventeen times. In four of these cases the term occurs in statements about the future restoration when Israel will be the true and proper people of God (1:11; 2:1, 23). In the remaining thirteen cases (from 1:9 to 11:7), however, what is said about the "people" (most often, "my people") is that they are in one way or another evil, deserving of punishment. An example would be that of 4:5: "my people perish for lack of knowledge," or 10:14, "the tumult will rise against your people." When Hosea speaks of sin, disobedience, rebellion, and wickedness, it is usually "you" (plural or collective) or "they" who have done it; the verbs and pronouns in such contexts are in the plural much more often than in the singular. Frequently it is simply "Israel" or "Ephraim" or the like that are said to have sinned and to be deserving of judgment. In these and other ways, Hosea, like other prophets, frequently preaches God's condemnation of an entire society as a unit.

The sins of any individual are not noted, except for a special analogical purpose, that is, the command about Hosea's second wife, mentioned in chapter 3 but not by name, whom he married after she had committed adultery and with whom he did not consummate the marriage (3:3).[7] Otherwise, if sin is mentioned in the Book of Hosea, it is corporate sin.

Frequently the corporate sin Hosea prophecies about is national sin—that of the Northern Kingdom or, several times, of Judah (4:15; 5:5, 10-14; 6:4, 11; 8:14; 10:11; 12:2). Occasionally, a smaller group is in view. The priests (4:4, 9; 5:1; 6:9) or the prophets (4:5; 9:7-8) are condemned as a group for their sins and/or for their complicity in the people's rebellion against God. On some occasions, corporate sin is identified in a city, such as Gilead (6:8; 12:11), Gilgal (9:15; 12:11), or Bethel (called in Hosea Beth-Awen; e.g., 10:5). "Gilead is a city of evildoers," says 6:8. "If Gilead is evil, what worthlessness they are!" says 12:11.

This does not mean that Hosea was unaware of individual sin. It means simply that God's message through the prophet was directed to a people, not to individuals, and concerned the fate of that people, rather than the fate of individuals. Rarely, prophets were inspired to prophecy about the fates of individuals, as in Amos's words to Amaziah about the fate of that priest and his family. Amos 7:17 records Amos's prediction of Amaziah's exile—which, however, ends with a statement about the exile of the whole nation of Israel, obviously the more significant point.

The theological question most commonly raised by mention of corporate sin is this: Is it fair that God should judge an entire group when surely some of its individual members were not party to the sins being judged? The answer to this question is, in one sense, by definition yes, since it is God's behavior that sets the standards of what is fair and what is not. The answer, however, should also be yes from the standpoint of a reasonable understanding of God's verbal revelation. We are told that he punishes people for their own sins, not those of others (e.g., Ezek 18; 33:1-20). Thus whatever he does with regard to corporate punishment for corporate sins will not preclude his being fair to individuals. Equity for individuals, however, often takes on an eschatological frame rather than a this-world frame, as much of Scripture (including but hardly limited to Job, Hebrews, 1 Peter, and Revelation) makes very clear. God's servants have no right to expect this life to be fair. They can expect only that the widespread unfairness of this life will be overturned and compensated for by the final judgment and the rewards of eternity.

Biblical statements about punishment for corporate sin fit this standard. They do not assume that innocent people escape the general punishment imposed upon the general populace of a nation or city or group. They are realistic, since life has always held such risks—for example, for innocent women and children in war or for livestock in severe drought or famine (Hos 4:3). They never suggest that the temporary miseries of this life, which itself is by definition temporary, constitute a final judgment of God. Israel's geopolitical judgment in ancient times, or the temporal judgment of its priests or prophets as a group, or any other corporate punishments, are essentially limited. Only the final judgment has the ability to separate out individual sin from corporate sin and thus impose appropriate punishments of everlasting duration.

That Israel's corporate punishments as announced by prophets like Hosea are not permanent is obvious in the expectation of restoration that surrounds such predictions. That all prophets were not corrupt even though condemned in group terms is obvious from the fact that Hosea

Corporate and Individual Sin

and others like him (Amos, etc.) were exceptions to the prevailing prophetic corruption. All citizens were surely not actually involved in idolatry and other forms of covenant breaking, as suggested by the fact that Hosea's words were preserved by people who apparently revered their call to be separate from the prevailing pattern of sin. And so on.

Nevertheless, much of the world's sin is corporate, rather than merely individual—societally patterned and accepted sin, sufficiently pervasive that the society (or subsection thereof) "as a whole" or "on balance" is seen as wicked. Hosea's preaching reflected this at virtually every turn: The "land of Israel has gone thoroughly into prostitution" (1:2). Sinful Israel is treated as a single unit, corporately personified as Yahweh's prostituting wife (2:2–15). "Ephraim is in league with idols" (4:17). Of Israel as a whole, God says, "your sins are so many, your hostility so great" (9:7).

If there is corporate sin, influencing individuals to partake in the group's corruption, there is also the promise of corporate redemption, inviting individuals to reject the prevailing evil and submit themselves to God's will looking forward to being part of a redeemed people:

> Let us return to Yahweh,
> For he has torn us apart, yet he will heal us;
> he has attacked us yet he will bandage us. (6:1)

> What will Ephraim have to do any more with idols?
> I will have responded and I will bless him. (14:8)

It must surely be stated that these corporate promises no more guarantee life for people born into a group than the corporate curses condemn innocent individuals to a negative eternal fate. There is a natural merit in, even a necessity of, speaking of nations and groups as corporate unities. This by no means negates individual responsibility. In our age of emphasis on individual rights, the Bible's strong representation of corporate sin—and redemption—provides a welcome corrective.

Guilt and guiltiness

Much modern Western psychological thinking differs from biblical revelation on the matter of guilt. Some forms of psychotherapy and perhaps most popular psychologizing advocate the value of introspection as one vehicle for the supposedly therapeutic release of harmful guilt. It has been pointed out by certain scholars that this notion of guilt—as an internalized psychological disposition affecting one's mental state and behavior—is not what the Bible means by guilt.[8] Biblically, guilt is not how you (rightly or wrongly) may feel about yourself or your life; guilt is guiltiness—trouble not with yourself but with God.

From the Book of Hosea it is clear that Israel had no trouble with guilty feelings—what many moderns think of when they hear the word "guilt." Israel, indeed, might have benefitted from some such feelings, in light of the fact that her behavior was deserving of punishment. Instead of advocating a therapeutic release of his people's guilt feelings, God through Hosea says:

> Ephraim's iniquity is wrapped up,
> his sin is stored up. (13:12)

Of the attitude of the people, God says it is sinful and deserving of punishment:

> Their heart is deceptive.
> Now they incur guilt. (10:2)

Only repentance can save the nation. God will temporarily abandon them until such time as they turn from their guilty behavior to him, repentant:

> I will go back to my place
> until they suffer for their guilt and seek me.
> When in trouble they will search me out. (5:15)

The concept of guilt, or guiltiness, is most commonly expressed via the word 'šm in Hebrew. Another Hebrew term, dām, can refer to guilt as well, the guilt that comes from harming others. It means literally "blood," but has a range of meaning that covers our English notions of "bloodshed," "death," and "murder," as well as "blood-guilt." It is used in this latter sense in Hos 12:14:

> His Lord will leave his blood-guilt upon him
> and will repay him for his contempt.

This statement leads to another about Israel's guilt, found in the very next verse of the prophecy:

> Truly he has spoken terror against Ephraim,
> he has raised his voice against Israel:
> "Because he has incurred guilt with Baal, he must
>   die." (13:1)

We note that Israel's guilt is never described as a matter of their own imagination; they all too often saw nothing wrong with their behavior. Instead, part of Hosea's prophetic responsibility was to teach the people that they were genuinely guilty. His preaching was intended to raise their awareness of their guilt, which was real, and dangerous to them—not from the standpoint of their emotional health, but from the standpoint of the wrath of God. His message to them was not to "let it out" but to cut it out: "As for you, Israel, do not incur guilt from Yahweh!" (4:15).

Yahweh's "wife" and "child"

Many ancient and modern religions are sexually dualistic in their view of deity. They believe that both male and female gods exist, and that many, if not all of them, are paired. In some instances the pairing is a marriage; in others it is what we might call cohabitation—or even an affair.

Such dualism is absolutely foreign to the teaching of the Bible. The dualistic magical practices of the Canaanites, such as "marrying" seed sown in fields in an effort to increase crop yields, or "marrying" cloth in clothing in an effort to stimulate the fertility of flax or sheep (Lev 19:19), or boiling a male goat kid in his mother's milk (Exod 23:17) were strictly outlawed, as was ritual sex in worship, also essentially dualistic (see above, The Attractions of Idolatry). The worship of any god other than Yahweh was forbidden, and this certainly included the worship of a goddess (cf. Exod 34:13; Deut 12:3). To the dualistic Canaanites, on the other hand, it was illogical to think that their god Baal would be celibate. He had to have a consort, whom we know as Asherah (Judg 3:7; 1 Kgs 18:19).

Since most of the Israelites during most of their history were not orthodox followers of the revealed truth, but apostatized idolaters, it is reasonable to imagine that at least some of them would corrupt the worship of Yahweh in the style of dualistic Canaanite religion, and begin to believe that Yahweh ought to have a goddess consort, too. This did, indeed, happen (cf. Deut 16:21; 2 Kgs 23:6). Extrabiblically, inscriptions and paintings found at the Sinai wilderness shrine of Kuntillet Ajrud prove that some Israelites from about the time of Hosea worshiped "Yahweh and his Asherah."[9] That is, they simply borrowed Baal's goddess girlfriend and gave her also to Yahweh. It wasn't orthodox, but neither were they. It was dualistic, forbidden by the Mosaic Law, but believed and practiced nevertheless.

What about the true biblical view of Yahweh? Obviously he was not married to a goddess nor cohabiting with one. Nevertheless, there is a sense in which he had a wife—though not a divine wife and not a literal wife. Yahweh's "wife" was, metaphorically, Israel, his people (cf. Isa 54:6; Jer 3:1; etc).

Hosea reflects this metaphorical marriage especially in chapters 1–3. Some scholars operating from an essentially antisupernatural bias have assumed that the origin of these chapters was in Hosea's own experience with an unhappy marriage, which he then projected upon Yahweh and Israel in a theological manner. In fact, we have no reason to think that Hosea's marriages (mentioned in Chs 1 and 3) were unhappy. Yahweh's metaphorical marriage was, however, very unhappy, and it is the subject of the elegant allegorical divorce story in 2:2–15 in which Israel is cast in the role of a woman who keeps cheating on her husband, that is, relying on other gods instead of Yahweh. In that passage, she is charged by Yahweh in a symbolic divorce proceeding: "Make the accusation that she is not my wife and I am not her husband" (2:2). She is called a "disgrace" (v 5); one who has taken "lovers" (vv 5, 7, 10, 12, 13); and Yahweh is called her "first husband" (v 7). To win her back he will "romance her" (v 14). She, happily, will eventually "respond . . . as she did when she was young," that is, when Israel in the wilderness did not yet know the allures of the gods of Canaan and thought only of the Lord.

Hosea makes other, much briefer, allusions to the metaphorical marriage of Israel and her God (e.g., 4:15; 8:9). The concept is found in many other parts of Scripture as well (e.g., Ps 45; Ezek 16), particularly in its New Testament form, where the church is the virgin "bride of Christ" (2 Cor 11:2; Eph 5:25–26; Rev 19:7; 21:20; 22:17) emphasizing, in contrast to Israel's infidelity, a chaste people ready for eternal "marriage" to God.

The other common family relationship metaphor, used in the Bible to express the dependency of Israel on God, is that of "father" and "child" or "son." This kind of language is used in the New Testament in a considerably more literal sense to describe the adoption into the family of God that the believer in Christ is privileged to enjoy (e.g., Rom 8:16–21; Gal 3:26; Eph 1:5). Much less common, however, is the metaphorical identification of the people of God in a corporate sense as God's "child" in the singular. Exod 4:22 ("Israel is my firstborn son . . . Let my son go") is probably the backdrop for Hosea's employment of this rare metaphor in 11:1:

> When Israel was a child I loved him.
> Out of Egypt I called my son.

As a classic instance of *sensus plenior* ("fuller meaning") in prophecy, this verse's unusual wording referred not only to the exodus from Egypt of the nation Israel, but of the exodus from Egypt of the embodiment and savior of that nation, Jesus Christ.

Two verses later (11:3), Hosea returns to the father-child metaphor in a poignant illustration of the love of God shown unstintingly to his offspring from the beginning of the stubborn child's life:

> It was I who taught Ephraim to walk,
> taking them by the arms;
> but they were not aware that I restored them to
> health.

Israel was a wayward wife, a rebellious child. Fortunately for his people, God was a husband who knew how to lovingly punish and restore, and a father who knew how to lovingly discipline and make secure forever.

The distant past and the ultimate future: the long view on Israel

Hosea's original audience heard him preach during the years from about 760 to about 722 B.C. Much of his inspired message concerned the situation in those decades in the Northern Kingdom. He also assumed some ability on the part of his audience to appreciate their history as a people, both in the recent and the distant past, as well as their ultimate future. The past was, of course, a given, a matter of common knowledge. The future was another matter, though in general terms just as knowable as the past to those who had faith in the true God and listened to his prophets.

Orthodox Israelites, few though they were, had an advantage in looking at both their past and their future. It had long ago been revealed. Already through Moses the story of the nation, from beginning to end, had been told. The Israelites of the generation born in the wilderness had heard the sweep of history, including the basic account of Israel's rescue from Egypt, the wandering in the wilderness, the conquest of the promised land, the long tenure in that land, their eventual destruction as a nation and exile for sin, their return from exile and resettlement, and their restoration as a new people in the Lord's new kingdom. The sweep of Israel's history is told in several places in the Pentateuch, but most systematically in Deut 1-4, and succinctly in Deut 4:20-31, where the entire period from the captivity in Egypt to the New Covenant is summarized.

All the prophets reflect this perspective. Some prophetical books, usually the longer ones, display knowledge of it routinely. In others, mostly the shorter books, the Pentateuchal outlines of Israel's past, present, and future are obviously assumed, even if not overtly displayed. In this regard, Israel is seen as a continuum in the Old Testament (and indeed all the more so in the New Testament, where the church is the automatic heir to the Old Testament promises to Israel; Gal 3:29). Every generation may be referred to as "you" whether in the past, present, or future from the point of view of the speaker and audience. Each generation is identified with all the others. The generation of the Exodus is also the generation of the exile. And so on. (Cf. the pronouns in Deut 4:20–31.)

This general sense of history is richly illustrated in Hosea's many references to the past and future. His audience hears about events of times to them long past as well as some more recent to their own era, and also about events for them—and to some extent for us—yet to come.

Particular attention is paid to the past in the "retrospective" section of the book (after 9:9), although this is only a matter of degree and not of kind. In 11:8, the Abrahamic-era ruin of Admah and Zeboiim (i.e., around 2000 B.C.) is mentioned. These cities were neighbors to Sodom and Gomorrah, and shared in their destruction, described in Gen 19. Hosea also makes use of parts of Jacob's story (1750 B.C.?), in 12:3, 4, 12. God's guidance and protection of his people has a long history, and reference to Jacob helps remind Hosea's audience of that fact. The Exodus of Israel from Egypt (ca. 1440 B.C.) is something Hosea mentions often 2:15; 9:10; 11:1; 12:9; 13:4), as many of the other prophets do. It was a point of contact with the belief, limited as it was, in Yahweh on the part of the people to whom the prophets preached. Israelites may have had distorted views of Yahweh and may not have worshiped him properly, especially in the North, but they all knew the story of the Exodus. The prophets were inspired again and again to remind people that the God they represented was the one who brought the nation into being in the first place.

Moses (12:13) and the wilderness wandering of the people's ancestors (12:9; 13:5) were topics in Hosea's preaching. He referred as well to the incident at Baal-Peor in Moab, which took place just before the conquest of Canaan (ca. 1400 B.C.), while the Israelites were at the end of that wilderness period (Hos 9:13; cf. Num 25). The story of Achor's rebellion (Josh 7) is alluded to in 2:15, as is the settlement and early history of the tribes in the days of Joshua (Hos 9:13; 10:1; 11:3–4). The account in Judg 19 of the homosexuals' sadistic gang rape at Gibeah, one of the most outrageous crimes in the nation's history, is referred to in 9:9 and 10:9. It should be understood that the crime itself was greatly compounded by the unwillingness of the people of Benjamin to punish those responsible, thus indicating the level of immorality tolerated during the days of the Judges. To this level, Hosea says Israel has once again sunk. The demand of the people at the end of the Judges period (i.e., ca. 1050 B.C.) for a king is also recalled, in 13:10 (cf. 1 Sam 8).

Later events—though still prior to Hosea's day—are mentioned also. A long history of worship at the heterodox but highly popular worship center of Gilgal over the years is taken for granted in 9:15. Years of alliances and attempted alliances with Egypt and Assyria form the backdrop for statements made in 5:13; 7:11; and 8:9. The history of prophetic attempts to call the people back to Yahweh is behind part of 12:10:

> I spoke through the prophets,
> I gave them many revelations
> and by the prophets I gave parables.

In 1:4, Hosea brings his audience's remembrance back to Jehu's massacre of the Israelite and Judean royal families in 842, nearly a century before. In 10:14, he speaks of "Shalman's destruction of Beth-Arbel," something we do not otherwise know about, but probably an event of scandalous brutality in the recent memory of Hosea's audience.[10]

The near future is the subject of so much of Hosea's preaching, the content of which has already been discussed above, that we need not elaborate on that here. The full range of the covenant curses, including but hardly limited to conquest by a foreign power and exile, was what Israel could expect soon enough (beginning with the Assyrian exile in 722 B.C.). The distant future, however, was also part of the purview of the divine revelation through Hosea. Israel would spend "many days" in captivity (3:4), deported to a foreign land for their sins (e.g., 10:10). This foreign land is often referred to by the metonymy "Egypt," with or without the added clarification that the actual term of exile would be served in Assyria (7:16; 8:13; 9:3, 6; 11:5). The vast majority of the nation would not survive its conquest and exile, but would die, as metaphorically related in 4:16:

> Yahweh will pasture them
> Like a lamb in the "Expanse" [hell].

Exile would not be their end. A return from exile was part of God's great overarching plan for his people's history, and this, too, is addressed in the book. Hos 10:10-11 predicts the return from exile (begun in 539 B.C.; cf. Ezra 1), as does 1:10-11, where the eschatological reunification of the peoples of Israel and Judah into a single, united, true people of God is announced: "The Judahites and Israelites will unite. They will appoint themselves a single leader, and will come up from the land/be resurrected." A similar statement, openly Messianic, is made in 3:5: "Afterwards the Israelites will return to seek Yahweh their God and David their king. They will turn in fear to Yahweh and his goodness in the end times." Israel's great eschatological era of blessing is further described in 2:16-23 and 14:1-8, passages rich and ornate with adumbrations of the New Covenant age and beyond.

From 2000 B.C. (Admah and Zeboiim) to a time yet in the future for us, the long view on Israel was given. There was no excuse for anyone who listened to Hosea to fail to see the plan of God. Paul says with regard to his description of Christ's coming again, "Therefore encourage one another with these words" (1 Thess 4:18). From the past to the future, the history of the people of God has always been under the control of the God of that people. This was surely encouraging to the faithful who heard Hosea preach, just as it is to us who read his prophecies from the printed page.

3 JOEL

Widely represented in the civilizations of the ancient Fertile Crescent was the concept that truly great kings could win a war in a single day.[1] Lesser monarchs might require weeks, months, or years to conclude an armed conflict, but a mighty sovereign was one who could vanquish his enemies the same day he set out to do so. Woe to his enemies on the day that he chose to attack! They would be defeated, his rule over them quickly established, and their fortunes thus suddenly reversed. From the point of view of the great sovereign's faithful subjects or allies, what a complete change was possible in just a day! They could go from oppression by their enemies to rescue, from humiliation to exaltation, from danger to peace and freedom—all in the time it takes the sun to make its circuit in the heavens.

For Israel, Yahweh was their great sovereign who could win his wars in a day, and thus who could deliver Israel from all its foes any time he chose to. Even in their many compromises with idolatry and polytheism, this notion of the power of the nation's historical God was still retained. It undoubtedly surfaced more prominently when military danger threatened, and may have been heard less in good times. Nevertheless, it remained a hope of the people, who genuinely believed that Yahweh would never abandon the nation he had brought out of Egypt and settled in Canaan. Having adopted the polytheistic thinking of their day, they saw no reason to think that the Lord should be offended if other gods were worshiped as long as he was worshiped, too. Thus they tended not to be aware that he was offended by their failure to worship him exclusively, and that as time had gone by he had become no longer a benign, protective sovereign, but their enemy. They kept looking for his "day" to come—a day when he would deliver them from the Assyrians or Babylonians, establish them as independent over their own affairs, and prosper them. What they did not realize was that his day would be instead a day of judgment for them.

Joel employs the phrase "Day of the Lord" (Hebrew *yôm yahweh*) five times, distributed fairly evenly through all three chapters of his prophecy (1:15; 2:1, 11, 31; and 3:14). The phrase does not occur incidentally. It is more like a title or summary phrase in each of its usages, and the subject matter that surrounds it is not unrelated, but in one way or another addresses the topic indicated by the phrase. In other words, the Day of the Lord is the subject of the Book of Joel.

Joel prophesied probably in the 590s or 580s B.C., as the Babylonians were closing in for the kill against Judah. His contemporaries, to whom he preached, knew well the concept of the Day of the Lord, and undoubtedly identified with it in the usual manner—thinking that it would represent deliverance for Israel and defeat for her foes, namely, the Babylonians. Prophets like Amos had tried to warn prior generations that for them the day would bring punishment, not deliverance, because they had made themselves the Lord's enemies by breaking his covenant (e.g., Amos 5:18–27). It had mostly fallen on deaf ears, and the generation that comprised Joel's audience was at any rate more likely to concentrate their attention on Isaiah's famous prediction of the Day of the Lord as a time of punishment for the Babylonians (Isa 13:6, 9). Yes, the day would indeed bring Babylon to wailing—but the day reserved for Israel would be just as bad.

Joel does not suggest that there would be only one Day of the Lord. Any time the Great King intervenes decisively in human history to war against his enemies, it can be termed a Day of the Lord. Joel's words point to both a near-time (for him) day and a more distant, eschatological day. This is consistent with the rest of Scripture, where several Days of the Lord can be identified. The fall of the North in 722 was one such day (Amos 5) as was the fall of the South in 586 (Ezek 13:5) as was the coming of Christ (Mal 4:5) as will be his second coming (1 Thess 5:2; 2 Pet 3:10). Great turning points in the plan of God are Days of the Lord, because they represent decisive victories of God in our fallen world.

In the first part of the Book of Joel (1:1 to 2:17), the Day of the Lord refers to that day when Israel will be conquered by armies doing the Lord's bidding. In the second part of the book, including 2:31 and 3:14, the Day of the Lord is a later one, that is, the eschatological day when the evil powers of the world, including the nations governed by them, will be defeated and the righteous vindicated.

Joel's first pericope, 1:1–20 is a call to lament because of the Babylonian invasion (likened to a locust plague). It warns of the disasters that will accompany the Day of the Lord that is coming in the near future for Judah. Verse 15 says:

> Woe for the day!
> For Yahweh's Day is near.
> It comes as a mighty ruin from the Almighty.

The Day of the Lord

The book's second self-contained passage, 2:1–17, is similar. Again, the invaders are compared to locusts, though it is clear that "the Lord's army" (v 11) is no group of insects. In this passage the Day of the Lord is clearly the topic, and the phrase itself is mentioned twice. The first instance is at the outset of the chapter:

Blow the horn in Zion,
Sound the alarm on my holy mountain.

Let everyone that lives in the land tremble,
Because the Day of Yahweh is coming, because it is
    near,

The day of darkness and gloom,
The day of clouds and blackness.

Like the dawn spreading across the hills is the
    populous, strong nation.
Nothing like it has existed from ancient times,
Nor will it again for generation after generation.
                                        (2:1–2)

The second instance is at 2:11:

Yahweh has raised his voice before his army!
How very great is his encampment!
How strong are those who carry out his words!

How great is the Day of Yahweh
And very fearful! Who can endure it?

In both instances, as throughout the passage, the Day of the Lord refers to the time of an overwhelming invasion of an enemy nation, whose troops do the Lord's bidding and whose purpose is to crush Israel. The proper response on the part of the people is repentance (vv 12–17), though there is every likelihood that Joel's audience for the most part did not think they needed any.

Joel is organized, like some of the other prophetical books (e.g., Ezekiel and Amos), in a woe-weal pattern, with judgments for past and present sins dominating the early part (1:1–2:17) and promises of postexilic restoration dominating the latter part (2:18–3:21). As we might expect, then, the final two references to the Day of the Lord are in the context of hope for the glorious future that the Lord has planned for those who belong to him:

> The sun will be turned into darkness
> And the moon into blood
> Before the coming of the Day of Yahweh,
> Great and fearful.
>
> And everyone who calls on the name of Yahweh will
>   be saved,
> because there will be escape in Mount Zion, that is,
>   Jerusalem, just as Yahweh has said, among the
>   survivors, whom Yahweh will call.
>
> (2:31–32)

This promise concludes the pericope (2:18–32) with a note of optimism for the eschatological future. The near future may involve great destruction and distress for Israel, but the eschaton will contain compensations for the faithful (including subjugation of their enemies, abundance, acceptance, the favor of God, the presence of his Spirit, etc.).

Joel's final use of the phrase Day of the Lord comes at 3:14:

> Mêlée! Mêlée in the valley of the verdict!
> For the Day of Yahweh is near in the valley of the
>   verdict!

The context is that of judgment upon all the nations, when Israel is vindicated and its foes on the world scene condemned by divine verdict. This verdict is essentially that of what we would call the final judgment, and the picture of the everlasting prosperity of the Lord's people in vv 17–21 is essentially that of the new heavens and new earth, including the new Jerusalem (cf. Gal 4:26; Heb 12:22; Rev 21:2ff.) still to come.

The prophetic lament

People who lived in ancient Israel heard laments a great deal. They heard funeral laments regularly, because their age was one when death was frequent and funeral processions a common part of life. They also heard lament psalms sung in worship, since that practice, too, was a part of daily life. Some prophetic laments are of the psalm type, in which an appeal is made to God for rescue from distress, and trust in God's ultimate goodness is expressed.[2] The majority of laments in the Old Testament prophetical books, however, are funeral laments, with a structure and subject matter parallel to those laments that were sung for departed loved ones. A parade example of the Old Testament funeral lament is David's lament over Saul and Jonathan (2 Sam 1:19–27) after they were slain defending Israel against the Philistines.

The prophets often sang laments for Israel or its enemies. These were usually proleptic, anticipating a future time when the nation in question would meet its doom. Some are caustically critical of the nation lamented, the funeral being an occasion for rejoicing on the part of the people of God that an oppressor nation will have been eliminated from the earth. Ezekiel is especially known for his mock funeral laments over Israel (e.g., Ezek 19) and various foreign nations (e.g., Tyre [ch 27]; Egypt [ch 30]). Amos's predictive lament over the fall of Israel in Amos 5:17 and Isaiah's taunting lament over the fall of the king of Babylon in Isa 14:4-23 are among other lengthy examples of this prophetic form of structuring a message from God.

Funeral laments had four typical ingredients in addition to whatever elements made the lament specific to a given person or group: (1) a call to mourning, (2) a eulogy for the now or future dead, (3) direct address to the now or future dead, and (4) a statement of the greatness of the tragedy to those who survive the departed. The first pericope of the Book of Joel (1:2-20) contains these elements to one degree or another, and may thus be classified as a lament, or somewhat more specifically because of its particular characteristics, a call to lament.

In Joel 1:2-20 the lament form may be outlined as follows:

vv 2-3	Call to mourning, with direct address to those involved
v 4	Greatness of the tragedy to the survivors
vv 5-7	Call to mourning (drunkards) and further description
vv 8-10	Call to mourning (general) and further description
vv 11-12	Call to mourning (farmers) and further description
vv 13-18	Call to mourning (priests) and further description
vv 19-20	Appeal to the Lord and further description of the tragedy

Inherent in the descriptions of the tragedy is the element of "eulogy" since the formerly abundant land, repeatedly referred to, is now laid waste. The land was the people's basic financial resource. If its vineyards were ruined (vv 5, 7, 10) or its fig trees stripped bare (v 7) or its fields desolated (v 10) or its olive trees wrecked (v 10) or its grain and fruit produce cut off (vv 11, 12) everyone would suffer. Not only plant life is "eulogized" in the passage; the enemy invasion has wrecked the all-important stored grains and fruits (v 17) and has denied food to the animals, both large and small cattle (v 18).

How could an enemy invasion do all this? The answer is found in appreciating the interaction of human and divine warfare. Human armies did their part, in the ancient equivalent of what in modern times is called a "scorched earth policy." Armies seized whatever they needed to eat, salted land that was under cultivation to prevent those they were conquering from using it again (cf. Judg 9:45), burned fields (cf. Judg 15:4-5), and filled in water sources (cf. 2 Kgs 3:19, 25). This invasion was also the work of God—he fought, too (2:1, 25). Unleashing the curses of the Mosaic covenant against Judah,[3] God added to the work of their conquerors by bringing about a drought, so that the usually available countryside areas of pasturage (vv 18, 19) and the water sources (v 20) were dry. Joel and the Judeans of his time had much, indeed, to lament. Their funeral was at hand. Death, the essential final curse of the covenant, was closing in on them because of their sins

Conquest, human and divine

The Day of the Lord is the central, indeed, exclusive, topic of the Book of Joel. Since the Day of the Lord derives from the concept of decisive war conquest, much in Joel will obviously be about conquest. There are in fact three types of conquest that are described in one way or another in the book: (1) a foreign nation's conquest of Israel (i.e., the Babylonian conquest of the 580s B.C.), (2) Yahweh's divine conquest of Israel, Yahweh being at the head of his "army," a force clearly not limited to human warriors, and (3) Yahweh's divine eschatological conquest of the nations who had once oppressed Israel, this conquest now rescuing rather than punishing Israel.

We have noted already that Joel's lament in chapter 1 describes some of the results of the attack of Israel's human foe in a manner that also focuses on the concomitant role of Yahweh as Israel's divine foe. Another way of expressing this is to say that no nation conquered Israel, whether partially or entirely, whether temporarily or permanently, of its own initiative. God, who controls the events of nations, was always behind any conquest of Israel. Indeed, he was always behind any conquest of Israel's foes. Israel never won or lost a battle on its own. When it came to war involving Israel, the Lord was fighting, too.

Israel itself had once been a conquering nation on God's behalf. It had defeated the Canaanites in fulfillment of God's decision, already revealed to Abraham in Gen 15, that the immoral Canaanite culture of the promised land must be eliminated. As a conquering people, however, Israel was still only a token fighting force. Its army under human leadership could nevertheless be termed God's army (e.g., 1 Sam 17:36), and it succeeded only because God also had his own heavenly army that actually did the fighting that really counted (cf. Judg 5:20).

The Old Testament contains many references to God's fighting for Israel, on the clear premise that Israel would have no chance on its own to win in battle without the Lord's supernatural aid:

The Lord will fight for you; you need only to be still. (Exod 14:14)

The Lord your God, who is going before you, will fight for you, as he did for you in Egypt. (Deut 1:30)

For the Lord your God is the one who goes with you to fight for you against your enemies to give you victory. (Deut 20:4)

Conquest, Human and Divine

For the battle is not yours, but God's. (2 Chr 20:15)

Sometimes biblical references to battle do not even mention
Israel but describe the action as entirely the Lord's, so central is his support, and so essential to earthly success is his
cosmic victory:

The Lord will march out like a mighty man, like a war-
rior he will stir up his zeal; with a shout he will raise the
battle cry and will triumph over his enemies. (Isa 42:13)

I will, however, have compassion on the family of Judah.
I will save them by Yahweh their God, but will not save
them by bow, by sword—by warfare—by cavalry, by
chariotry. (Hos 1:7)

The Lord will go out and fight against those nations, as
he fights in the day of battle. (Zech 14:3)

In Joel, the conquering Babylonians are depicted as a human
army impressive in its sheer numbers:

. . . a nation has invaded my land,
strong and innumerable . .   (1:6)

Like the dawn spreading across the hills is the
    populous, strong nation.
Nothing like it has existed from ancient times,
Nor will it again for generation after generation. (2:2)

It also becomes evident that the Babylonians are merely the
visible representation of a heavenly army led by Yahweh:

Yahweh has raised his voice before his army!
How very great is his encampment!
How strong are those who carry out his words! (2:11)

And the Lord calls his forces of destruction: "My great army which I sent among you" (2:25).

Joel's most obvious reference to the direct warfare of God against the nations of the world who oppose Israel and therefore God himself is found in the eschatological battle/judgment scene of 4:1–21, and particularly verses 9–16. We note in this passage no mention that Israel's human forces would even be involved in the defeat of the nations. Instead, those who had once conquered Israel will be defeated in battle and judged directly by Yahweh, who will hand power back to Israel, after forcibly taking it from the human powers that once prevailed in the time of Joel.

After a call to the nations to prepare for war, with everyone required to fight (4:9–11), Yahweh invites—indeed commands—the nations to attack Israel in the Valley of Jehoshaphat (Jehoshaphat means "The Lord judges/has judged") where they will be defeated by Yahweh's supernatural power (vv 14–16). Having accomplished this, Yahweh will then restore Israel (vv 17–21) at the expense of these once great nations (e.g., Egypt, v 19). Here the conquest is of a future, divine sort, a conquest over human forces by the divine sovereign on behalf of the people of God.

Israel was virtually always puny compared to its foes. Unless Yahweh fought for his people, they really didn't stand a chance in battle. Left to their natural devices, their lot was to be conquered by others. This is exactly what happened to them in the early sixth century when Joel prophesied, and it happened because God made it happen. Their eventual restoration as a people was on the same order: left to their own devices they could not possibly have managed it. Because "Yahweh is a refuge for his people, a stronghold for the Israelites" (4:16), however, it would occur. Conquests of Israel by others, or of others by Israel, were always in the Lord's hands.

Conquest, Human and Divine

The Old Testament prophetical books come from a relatively brief period of time, from about 760 B.C. (Amos and Hosea) to about 460 B.C. (Malachi). These three centuries were times of upheaval. It was during this period that (northern) Israel and eventually Judah were conquered and exiled, so that God's people fell under the continuous domination of foreign empires, never again to live as an independent nation. Although three hundred years is a long time from the point of view of an individual lifetime, it is a short time from the point of view of the sweep of history, and the prophets had the sweep of history in mind when they preached.[4]

The prophets saw their day as the beginning of the end of the Old Covenant era. Theirs was a bad time, but God had revealed that the eventual future would be very different. Israel was degenerating, was in the process of being thrown out of the promised land by an angry God, and had no hope of escaping the divine wrath. There was nothing more to expect in the current age by way of divine blessing, national achievement, prestige among the nations of the world, etc. If the faithful among God's people were to have hope, it would be found in anticipation of the blessings of a new age to come, not in a return to the present order of things.

In other words, the fulfillment of Israel's potential for good in the eyes of the Lord was not in a mere rebuilding of current institutions or in a return to the status quo minus the Babylonians. It was, rather, in an entirely new era of history, in which God and his people would finally be united together as they always should have been but rarely were, in which after a turning point of great significance the people of God would know the Lord in fact rather than merely in name (cf. Jer 31:34).

Joel reflects repeatedly this concept that Israel's future was to be found not in the ways of the current age but in a new age, very different from the old and very distant from what was for him the present. The manner in which God would relate to his people in that new age would be different, the manner in which the people would behave would be different, and the place of God's people in the world would be different.

Joel's description of the new age begins at 2:18, which is a turning point in the book. After unleashing covenant curses to an extent that spells disaster for Israel, God will eventually turn to bless Israel. Joel 2:18 summarizes this expectation this way:

> But Yahweh has become jealous for his land
> And has taken pity on his people.

Joel calls what the Lord will do in the new age "something great" (2:20-21), a "twofold" restoration of what had been lost (2:25), a time of "miraculous things" (2:26), and an age when "never again will my people be put to shame" (2:27). It will be a time characterized, according to the restoration blessings of the Mosaic covenant, by such happy conditions as return from exile (3:2, 7, 20), agricultural bounty (2:19, 22, 23, 24, 26), and freedom from oppression by enemies (2:20, 25-26; 3:2, 9-16, 19-21).

In Joel, the new age to come is also characterized by three strong emphases: (1) the outpouring of God's spirit, (2) the changing of the world order by decisive divine intervention, and (3) the transformation of the status of the people of God from shame to exaltation.

The outpouring of God's spirit is the topic of 2:28-32, the famous passage quoted by Peter at Pentecost (Acts 2:17-21). Here is contained the prediction of one of the most significant changes from the Old Covenant to the New, the democratization of the Holy Spirit. In the Old Testament era the Spirit of God now and again "filled" (e.g., Exod 31:3) or "rested upon" (e.g., Num 11:25) particular individuals for a long or short time, but was not generally possessed by all of God's people (cf. Num 11:29). In the new age, however, God will pour out his spirit on "all flesh" (2:28)—male and female, old and young, slave and free (2:28-29). The true, eschatological Israel will finally be the kingdom of priests that it was called into existence to become (Exod 19:6), each representing the truth and power of God, each exercising his or her spiritual gifts to the glory of God.

This outpouring of the Spirit would constitute a Day of the Lord (2:31), a decisive day of divine intervention in history. Joel's poetic descriptions of the darkness of that day (2:30-31) are part of the common prophetic message about the Day of the Lord; it is not a day of business as usual, but a turning point. The coming of Christ was *the* turning point of the ages, providing as it did the opportunity that everyone who called on the name of the Lord could be saved (2:32). This meant a changing of the world order. Joel portrays that change further in 3:2-16, in which the defeat and final judgment of the powers opposed to God is vividly described. It will be a time when:

> The sun and moon have darkened,
> The stars have stopped their shining.
>
> Yahweh roars from Zion,
> He raises his voice from Jerusalem
> So that the sky and the earth shake. (3:15-16)

Finally, the new age will be characterized by the transformation of the status of the people of God. Shame among the peoples of the world was their standing in the years following Joel's prophecy. Humiliated in war, stripped of wealth and deported to foreign soil, they had little to take pride in. Through Joel, however, God reminds all those faithful to him at that time and in the future that he would "restore their fortunes" (Heb. Hêšîb š^ebût; 3:1). Acting on behalf of his people, his possession (3:2), God would turn the tables on the nations that had once oppressed them, giving them in kind what they had done to the Israelites (3:4–8), and thus giving his people refuge in him (3:16). The new station of God's people is centered prophetically on the new Jerusalem (3:17, 20), where holiness will prevail in contrast to the sin that caused Israel's problems in the first place, and where Yahweh will provide for the needs of his people (3:18) who will be free from threat of attack or domination by the powers of this world (3:17, 19, 21).

The Holy Spirit

Six prophets speak of the Holy Spirit: Isaiah (twelve times), Ezekiel (fourteen times), Joel (twice), Micah (twice), Haggai (once), and Zechariah (three times). Only Isaiah uses language that we would translate as "Holy Spirit," however. In Isa 63:10–11, God speaks of "my Holy Spirit," Heb. rûaḥ qodšî. Holy Spirit is more commonly a New Testament term which we nevertheless use appropriately to refer to the Spirit in the Old Testament as well.

The frequency of terms for Holy Spirit in the prophets may be summarized as follows:

Term	Occurrences in Prophetical Books
My Spirit	11
The Spirit	10
Spirit of the Lord	6
His Spirit	3
Holy Spirit	2
Spirit of the Lord Yahweh	1
Spirit of God	1

A term, of course, is not the same as a concept. What these figures show is that the concept of God's Holy Spirit may be understood as expressed via a variety of terms among the prophets, as long as it is also noted that the common denominator of all such terms is the Hebrew word *rûaḥ,* "spirit."

Obviously, Joel is not the only prophet who speaks of the Holy Spirit. He is also not the only prophet who speaks of the outpouring of that Spirit. Isaiah, for example, predicts the day when:

> the Spirit is poured upon us from on high,
> and the desert becomes a fertile field. (32:15)

He also quotes the Lord as saying:

> For I will pour water on the thirsty land,
> and streams on the dry ground.
>
> I will pour out my Spirit on your offspring,
> and my blessing on your descendants. (44:3)

Ezekiel, too, speaks of God's pouring out his Spirit:

> I will no longer hide my face from them, for I will pour out my Spirit on the house of Israel, declares the Lord Yahweh. (39:29)

What makes Joel's prophecy special in its prediction of the Spirit in the new age is its emphasis on three factors: the identity, the response, and the rescue of those who receive the Spirit. With regard to the identity of the recipients of the Spirit, Joel 2:28-29 effectively eliminates sexism, ageism, and discrimination based on social status from consideration in connection with the gift of the Spirit. "Sons and daughters," "old men," "young men," and "male slaves and female slaves" will all have the Spirit poured out on them. The age of the Spirit is characterized, truly, by a lack of distinction according to these categories as regards the work of God (cf. Gal 3:28). This surely does not mean, however, that all roles are blurred or abolished. Nothing in Joel 2 implies that in the age of the Spirit men and women are identical, that old and young are indistinguishable, or any such thing. It means that despite their distinctions, all people, of any age, class, or gender, are equal when it comes to the matter of possession of the Spirit in Christ.

They are also equal in potential of response to the Spirit. It would be absurd to suggest that Joel's words look toward an era when everyone will have all spiritual gifts, or even the category of gift addressed in 2:28-29, namely, prophecy. All *will* have something that Old Testament prophets did, however. All will experience the indwelling of the Spirit, who is a revealer of the things of God. Joel's stylized expression, involving "prophecy," "dreams," and "visions" is merely a synecdochic way of making the point that the Spirit age will see all believers related to God in the manner that the Old Covenant reserved in a more limited way, and for only a few. Jesus' words similarly accent the special privileges of the Spirit age: "Truly I say to you, among those born of women there has risen no one greater than John the Baptist; yet he who is least in the kingdom of heaven is greater than he" (Matt 11:11).

Rescue from destruction is the third advantage granted to those on whom the Spirit is poured out. This is the point of Joel 2:32, which promises: "And everyone who calls on the name of Yahweh will be saved, because there will be escape in Mount Zion, that is, Jerusalem, just as Yahweh said, among the survivors, whom Yahweh will call."

The statement at the end of this verse, that Yahweh will call "survivors," is an instance of the common position in the prophets, based on the panorama of history revealed in the Pentateuch, that Israel must first be decimated and exiled before a remnant can be redeemed. The age of the Spirit will, however, be characterized not merely by survival, but by abundance as the greater context, 2:18–32, demonstrates. This abundance will include salvation for all those who call on the Lord. When Joel's audience heard him preach that "everyone who calls on the name of the Lord will be saved" and that God's Spirit would be poured out "on all flesh" (v 28), some or many of them may have thought that this was a promise intended for Israelites only. Joel's words, however, speak of survivors of the Day of Yahweh, which is in Joel surely an event involving not merely Israel but "the nations" (4:2, 9, 12). From the position we who are in Christ occupy in the age of the Spirit, we know that it was certainly not merely Judeans or Israelites to whom the benefits spoken of in this passage would be applied by the very Spirit of whom it speaks.

4 AMOS

Yahweh's universal sovereignty

Yahweh was not a typical god. A typical god was worshiped via idols, and Yahweh would allow none of that. A typical god wanted to be given sacrifices without any concern for the ethical behavior of those who sacrificed to him or her. Not so with Yahweh, whose covenant demanded obedience to the highest ethical standards. A typical god was worshiped at shrines in all sorts of locations—the more the better. Yahweh insisted on being worshiped at only one location, Jerusalem. A typical god was worshiped frequently; every meat meal was part of the system of worshiping such gods or goddesses. Yahweh was to be worshiped in a more scheduled manner, with three major gatherings a year to constitute his nation's common worship obligation. And so on.[1]

A typical god was also thought to have limited power. The prevailing polytheism of the ancient world denied full power to any single god or goddess; power was shared by many gods, some with more, some with less, but none with all. A typical

63

Yahweh's Universal Sovereignty

god also tended to have limited geographical jurisdiction. The plural expression "the Baals" (e.g., 1 Kgs 18:18) alludes to this. Each Baal (Heb. for "lord") was thought to have influence in a particular region within Canaan. On a larger scale, each nation had its own national god: Chemosh in Moab, Hadad in Syria, Dagon among the Philistines, Marduk among the Babylonians, etc. No typical god, however, was the sovereign over all the world, supreme, with no rivals, no other gods having a share of his or her power—but then, Yahweh was not a typical god.

Foundational, nonnegotiable, intrinsic to the orthodoxy revealed to Israel at Mount Sinai was monotheism. The Book of Amos, ever consistent with that Law, portrays Yahweh as sovereign over not only Israel, and not only over all the nations, but over all creation, all individuals.

As "Yahweh of the Armies" (*yahweh ṣᵉbā'ôt*, usually translated "Lord of hosts"), he is supreme in heaven (3:13, etc.). The "armies" under his control are the host of heaven, well known from elsewhere in the Scripture as angels and "principalities and powers." Yahweh is also the creator and sustainer of the world, as evidenced in several places in Amos. For example, in the so-called hymn fragments (bits of a well-known Israelite hymn of the day, found in 4:13, 5:8, and 9:5–6, whose words Amos employed to remind the Israelites of what they were supposed to believe), Yahweh is "shaper of the mountains and creator of the wind," "who turns the dawn into darkness and walks the earth's heights" (4:13). He is also

> The one who made the Pleiades and Orion,
> Who turns darkness to dawn
> And darkens day into night,
>
> Who summons the sea's waters
> And pours them on the earth.
> Yahweh is his name! (5:8)

He is further described in the final fragment of the hymn as:

> The Lord, Yahweh of the Armies,
> Who touches the earth so that it crumbles,
> And all who live in it mourn,
>
> And all of it rises like the Nile
> And sinks like the Nile of Egypt;
>
> Who builds his upper chamber in heaven,
> And has founded his storeroom on the earth,
>
> Who summons the sea's waters
> And pours them out on the earth—
> Yahweh is his name! (9:5-6)

As creator and sustainer of the heavens and the earth, Yahweh is obviously also powerful over the events of nations. It is he who not only governs Israel and Judah, but also Syria (1:3-5), Philistia (1:6-7), Phoenicia (1:9-10), Edom (1:11-12), Ammon (1:13-15), and Moab (2:1-3). He will control their futures, see that they are destroyed at the time his judgment also destroys Israel and Judah, and exile their survivors just as he will exile the survivors of his own people. Yes, he has *a* people, but those who are not specifically that people are nonetheless fully under his control, even to the extent of bearing "his name" (9:12), that is, being his to dominate. This we should understand easily enough, since Christians would hardly believe that God has no power over non-Christians, or even *less* power over them than over those who acknowledge him as Lord.

Amos's inspired words pointed out that Yahweh ruled, for example, in North Africa, the Mediterranean islands, and Mesopotamia as well. In 9:7, an instance of this claim to universal sovereignty, he says: "Aren't you just like the

Nubians in relation to me, Israelites?—Oracle of Yahweh. Didn't I bring up Israel out of the land of Egypt, and the Philistines from Crete, and Aram from Kir?"

He has control over all territories and their populations. He causes earthquakes (the rising and falling of the land like that of the Nile; 9:5), which may be described as the effect of the roar of his voice (1:2). He determines the weather and thus the fertility of the land (e.g., 4:6-8; 1:2), crop pests (4:9; 7:1) as well as the course of disease in the population (4:10). He can, indeed, destroy the earth with fire (7:4). He can determine the future of the individual (7:11, 17) and of groups (e.g., 9:11-13). All of creation is under his sovereignty (e.g., 9:2-4).

For those opposed to him, there is no hope for escape of his judgment as 9:10 reminds: "All the sinners of my people will die by the sword, those who say, No harm will come near us or affect us." While for those who trust in him, his universal sovereignty is a great comfort. The promises of restoration and abundance that close the book (9:11-15) remind us of his great power to protect and provide, to bless and to heal, to guide the future of the nations and our own individual lives.

Social justice: the poor and the rich

Politically, it was the nation of Israel that constituted God's special people in Old Testament times. Economically, however, there was a sense in which it was the poor who belonged especially to him. Ps 14:6 states: "If the plans of the poor are frustrated, indeed Yahweh is his refuge." Ps 140:12 assures: "I know that Yahweh secures justice for the poor and upholds the cause of the needy." Isa 11:4 promises the following of the Messiah: "with righteousness he will judge the needy, with justice he will give decisions for the poor of the earth." Isa 25:4 praises God for being "a refuge for the poor, a refuge for the needy in his distress."

Among the minor prophets, none was inspired to pay more attention to the needs of the poor than Amos. The relationship of social justice to economic issues was surely a notable emphasis of his preaching. For example, in the book's opening attack on the sins of (northern) Israel for which it would be conquered and exiled, his first words identifying the injustices that prevailed in the North are:

This is what Yahweh said:

Because of the multiple crimes of Israel
I will not restore it;

Because they have sold the righteous for money
And the needy (Heb. ´ebyôn) in exchange for a pair of
    sandals.

They trample the heads of the poor (Heb. dallîm) into
    the dust of the earth,
And they keep the oppressed (Heb. `ᵃnāwîm) from
    getting anywhere. (Amos 2:6–7)

After mentioning the sin of cultic prostitution associated with idolatry (v 7b), Amos returns immediately to the topic of the oppression of the poor:

They stretch out on clothes taken as collateral,
Beside every altar.

They drink wine given to pay a fine,
At the house of their god. (Amos 2:8)

A most interesting fact about these charges against Israel is their contrast to the charges that parallel them in the earlier portions of Amos's long, carefully patterned oracle against the Syro-Palestinian nations in chapters 1 and 2.

Aram, Philistia, Tyre, Edom, Ammon, and Moab are all denounced for their vicious cruelties in or after wars, such as exterminating populations in border wars or selling populations into slavery (1:3–2:3). In the case of Judah and Israel, however, the places in the pattern of accusation reserved in the previous portions of the oracle for citation of heinous international crimes are filled by descriptions of violations of the Mosaic covenant, Yahweh's special law for his own people. What the other nations had done was a violation of Yahweh's implicit covenant with all the nations of the world, who, though lacking special revelation of his Law, nevertheless could be held to general standards of human decency and fairness (cf. Rom 1:18–32). What Judah (Amos 2:4–5) and Israel (2:6–16) had done, however, were subject to judgment according to the covenant revealed to them. In other words, such Israelite crimes as Amos cites are clearly just as odious as the pitiless savageries that other nations had been doing to each other in war.

What exactly had been happening in Israel to the poor? The answer is simply that they were being oppressed—used and abused for personal power and profit—by those more wealthy and powerful. The reference to selling the righteous and needy in verse 6 is an allusion to creditors' selling helpless debtors into slavery after foreclosing on loans. "Trampling the heads of the poor" and "keeping the oppressed from getting anywhere" (v 7) is a way of describing the systematic discrimination against the economically disadvantaged in Israel, who were routinely denied their rights by the courts, by the government, and by the well-to-do citizenry of the nation. The language of verse 8 about taking clothes as collateral and wine in fines refers to violations of the laws of Exod 22:25–27 and Deut 24:10–13, 17. Those laws prohibited excessive or confiscatory collateral for loans. In direct violation of the law, poor people had their outer clothing taken from them to ensure repayment, while in the meantime they suffered during the cold Palestinian nights. They were also fined heavily from their desperately needed crop harvests, such as their wine, to punish them for missed loan payment deadlines.

The divine Law, in order to protect the poor, had required that no interest could be charged by Israelites to their fellow citizens (Exod 22:25). Systematically violating this stipulation of the covenant, ruthless Israelites had not only been charging interest on loans, but also exacting cruel penalties for failure to repay. The poor, of course, were those most in need of loans from time to time, especially in cases of frugal harvests as a result of bad weather. Seizing upon the dependency of the poor on such loans, the exploiters saw a way to enrich themselves: lending during hard times at high interest rates, and then taking farms, houses (cf. Isa 5:8), produce, and even people for their own use or for resale whenever the poor could not repay. For such evils, overlooked by those who should have cared and openly practiced by those who didn't, the nation was to see calamity when the enemy invaded (Amos 2:13-16).

In Amos 4:1, we read of a leisure class in Israel, exemplified by wealthy, nonworking Samaritan women (a highly unusual thing in biblical times) who require their husbands to serve them ("Who say to their masters, 'Go get us something to drink.'"). Through Amos, God says that they "oppress the poor and crush the needy." How did they do this? They were able to grow wealthy and lazy because they had poor people working for them at miserable wages and under wretched conditions—people in at least some instances probably working on their own former farms now in the hands of their oppressors. In 5:11-12, Amos describes the process:

> Because when you get a judgment against the poor
> You take from him the produce of his field, . . .
>
> For I am aware of the frequency of your crimes
> And the severity of your sins—

Social Justice: The Poor and the Rich

Persecutors of the righteous, bribe takers,
Who reject the claims of the needy at the gate!

By controlling the legal system, paying bribes as necessary,
the rich could get richer at the expense of the poor by foreclosing on property and by obtaining crushing fines against
the poor, which had to be paid in produce from the fields
of the poor, produce then sold at very nice profits.

The oppression didn't stop there. As the increased urbanization of the nation resulted in the movement of more and
more people to the cities, a new opportunity for exploitation
of the poor was created. People who live on their own farms
or near those of friends or relatives can usually get food free
or buy food at "producer prices." Those removed from the
land in cities must usually pay middlemen, who may if un-
scrupulous jack up prices beyond fair profits, since the poor
of the city have little recourse but to pay to eat. They cannot
move back to the farms easily (farms that may have been
taken from them or their parents anyway) and cannot just
leave their jobs daily to walk out to the country to bargain
for food. So they must pay the city price—and take what
they get for their money. The whole process, from foreclo-
sure and debt slavery to inflated city prices for poor-quality
food is condemned in Amos 8:4-6:

Listen to this, you who trample on the poor,
Eliminating the oppressed people of the land, saying,

"When will the New Moon be over so that we can sell
grain,
And the Sabbath so that we can put wheat on sale,

So that we can shrink the ephah and increase the
shekel,
And cheat with inaccurate scales;

So that we can buy poor people for money,
A needy person for a pair of sandals,
And sell the sweepings in with the wheat?

Cheating people with small ephahs (grain measures), underweight shekels (roughly half-ounce weights), and rigged scales violated the law of God revealed in the Pentateuch (e.g., Lev 19:35–36). Amos, however, lived in a day when that law was scoffed at.

In Israel there was supposed to be no favoritism showed either to rich or to poor, but rather equal justice under the law (Lev 19:15). What Amos saw in Israel was just the opposite: rampant favoritism, unequal justice in the courts, exploitation of the poor whom God loved and for whom he had declared himself a special refuge. Is it any wonder, then, that Israel was bound for destruction as a nation? Indeed, Yahweh had sworn: "I will never forget all their deeds" (8:7).

The role of leadership in corporate sin

What made Israel turn away from the Lord? There were a variety of factors. Israel's apostasy was hardly a sudden or spontaneous development, as is clear in the long story of that apostasy told in the historical books of the Old Testament. Indeed, the prophets recognized that the tendency to rebel was always present,[2] just as the Pentateuch had long before adumbrated.[3] Among the many factors was one that could hardly be overlooked—leadership. Large groups of people don't usually act in a concerted fashion unless they are led. It may in fact be asserted that people do not normally even *drift* into the same sorts of sin, that is, sin that is so common as to constitute a national characteristic, as those denounced in the prophetical books, by accident. Actions reflecting a national mentality are undertaken not randomly, but in response

The Role of Leadership in Corporate Sin

to influences. A whole population does not just happen to decide to live a certain way, as if everyone at once independently got the same idea. Populations *respond* to ideas. They take hints from those who are influential. The many follow the lead of the few.

It is, in other words, highly unlikely that Israel as a nation would have rebelled so far from obedience to Yahweh's covenant if the nation's leadership had not aided and abetted the process. The leadership of the nation was not merely passively sharing the people's sin; it was helping it along.

There are four classes of leadership commonly mentioned in the Bible: kings, prophets, priests, and prominent citizens. All four are mentioned in Amos. Interestingly prophet, priest, and king are involved together in a single passage, the only biographical passage in the book, 7:10-17. It concerns an attempt by a priest, Amaziah, to keep a prophet, Amos, from preaching at the royal sanctuary of Bethel, by appealing to the king, Jeroboam II. In ancient Israel, kings controlled religious practices to a substantial degree. They appointed priests, selected sanctuaries, provided funds for temple upkeep and offerings, etc.[4] Amos's preaching at Bethel was clearly critical of the king: he was openly predicting the annihilation of the present dynasty, the conquest of Israel, and the exile of the population as a punishment for the nation's sins.

The high priest of the Bethel sanctuary, Amaziah, is quoted in 7:10-11 as reporting to the king that: "Amos has launched a conspiracy against you in the very heart of Israel. The land cannot contain everything he is saying! For here is what he said: 'Jeroboam will die by the sword and Israel will definitely be exiled from her native land.'" Although Amos had never said that Jeroboam himself would "die by the sword" but only that God would "rise up with a sword against Jeroboam's family" (7:9, a prophecy fulfilled via the assassination of Jeroboam's son, Zechariah, by Shallum; cf. 2 Kgs 15:8-12), Amaziah chose to word his message to the king in the most damaging way, hoping to get royal support for his attempt to expel Amos from the North to the prophet's southern homeland (7:12). Amaziah used as his justification for forbidding Amos to preach the argument that Bethel was in effect a personal, private protectorate of the king: "But don't do any more prophesying at Bethel because it is a royal sanctuary, a state temple" (v 13).

What Amaziah was doing is exactly the sort of thing an earlier prophecy of Amos had condemned Israelites for, that is, commanding (true) prophets not to prophesy (2:12). Who had the kind of authority that could prohibit a prophet from preaching? The national leadership did. We do not know whether Jeroboam confronted Amos directly or not, but he may well have moved to discourage Amos from staying in Israel by speaking quietly to business leaders about him. Amos was a traveling sheep breeder and sycamore fig cultivator rather than a professional prophet (7:14; cf. WBC 31:376-77). His business in the North may have been vulnerable to official pressure. He himself was obviously not inclined to back down to Amaziah's threats, and in response to them God gave him a defiant reply:

Now listen to Yahweh's word, you who say

'Do not prophesy against Israel,
Do not preach against the family of Isaac.'

Therefore here is what Yahweh has said:

'Your wife will become a prostitute in the city,
And your sons and daughters will fall by the sword.

The Role of Leadership in Corporate Sin

Your land will be divided up by a measuring line,
And you yourself will die in an unclean land.

Israel will definitely be exiled from its native land!'
                                                    (7:16-17)

As high priest at the dominant sanctuary of northern Israel,
Amaziah was a powerful, influential leader. Unquestionably,
Jeroboam the king was a leader. Orthodox prophets of the
Lord could also have been leaders against the prevailing
degeneration, if they had not been suppressed at this time, as
Amos's contemporary Hosea also confirms (Hos 9:7). False
prophets, on the other hand, were apparently given suffi-
cient rein to exert considerable influence, along with the
heterodox Northern priesthood, in leading the people astray
(cf. Hosea 4:5).

The fourth leadership group, the prominent citizenry, may
well have had an even greater role in keeping the nation in
sin than the other three. It may reasonably be assumed that
if large numbers of them had asserted themselves in favor
of keeping the Mosaic covenant, the king, the priests, and
the prophets would have been chastened. In fact the prominent citizenry pushed in the opposite direction—subtly and
steadily pressuring and/or inviting government and clergy to
drift away from fidelity to the nation's religious roots. In 3:10,
Amos speaks of "those who store up violence and destruction
in their royal fortifications." The Hebrew term ʾarmᵉnōth,
here translated "royal fortifications," refers to the fortress-
like citadels which housed residences and administrative
complexes, built at the heart of Israel's larger cities, where the
nobility and wealthy citizens lived. These were the people
who wielded the real power in the cities, and in the countryside as well—and they were no devotees of the Sinai
covenant (cf. 3:11; 4:1).

In 6:1-7, Amos preaches:

Woe to those comfortable in Zion,
And who feel secure on Mount Samaria,

Preeminent persons of the leading nation,
To whom the family of Israel come! (v 1)

These were members of a privileged, leisure class, who
could stay in bed when the ancient equivalent of their
horoscope was not positive (v 3). They had the money to
buy luxuries (vv 4, 6) and to indulge in idle pastimes (v 5).
Because of their influence for bad rather than good in the
nation, they would "go into exile at the front of the exiles"
(v 7). Those used to being first in influence would be first in
shame when the Lord's punishment was meted out. These
were people with both winter and summer houses, some
inlaid with ivory, mansions in a real sense of the term (3:15).
Their impressive cut-stone houses and lush vineyards (5:11)
were symbols of their rank, indications of their societal
supremacy. They were indeed leaders—leading Israel to
turn from God. God, however, was aware of the severity of
their sins (5:12) and would punish accordingly.

Divine prosecution of covenant violators

Amos 3:1–2 says of Israel:

Listen to this word that Yahweh has spoken against
you, Israelites, against the whole family I brought up
from Egypt:

> I have known only you
> Of all the families of the earth.
> Therefore I will punish you
> For all your sins.

This brief prose introduction and poetic quatrain summarize the implications of the Lord's special relationship to his Old Testament chosen people. Because they enjoy his personal care, they also cannot escape his personal attention to their need for punishment under his covenant.

A covenant is a law, and anyone who breaks a covenant may be considered a lawbreaker. God's covenant with Israel was a law, and when Israel broke that covenant, they were in danger of punishment. A law without penalties would be a sham of a law. The violator of the law must pay. Because this understanding of law fit the situation of the people of Israel in relation to God's covenant, the prophets frequently were inspired to imagine Israel as a defendant hauled into court and charged with crimes. They imagined the prosecutor in the court case to be Yahweh, Israel's God. He would cite the evidence against his sinful people, and they would have no recourse but to await the verdict of the judge.

Who was that judge? He, too, was Yahweh. Having come to his decision, he rendered a verdict. Who enforced the verdict? Yahweh did that as well. Obviously the outcome of the case against Israel was clear from the start, since the Lord Almighty could hardly be hoodwinked by his people—but that is part and parcel of what we call the "covenant lawsuit" form in the prophets.[5]

Such lawsuits commonly contain the following components. First, there is usually some kind of reference to a summons to justice, that is, to appear in court. Then the judge (God) speaks. He addresses the defendant Israel directly, proves the guilt of the defendant by evidence, and utters a judgment sentence. These components may occur in a variety of arrangements, but the order we have just described is common.

Amos 3 contains two such covenant lawsuit scenes, both brief and blunt. The first is in verses 1-2, cited above, where "Listen . ." assumes that the nation has been brought into court to hear the case against them. The Israelites are then addressed directly, their sins are described as plentiful ("all your sins") and their judgment (broad, general punishment) is announced. Typically in the prophets, the judgment sentence is introduced by "therefore" (most often Heb. 'alkēn or lākēn) as in the third line of the quatrain in verse 2. Thus these two short verses contain the digest of a court scene in which the guilty nation as defendant is tried, convicted, and sentenced by the divine judge.

Amos 3:9–11 contains another such literary form, this time imagining the great nations of the day, Assyria and Egypt, as expert court witnesses to Israel's evil, in the it-takes-one-to-know-one vein. This lawsuit reads as follows:

Announce it at the royal fortifications in Assyria
And at the royal fortifications in the land of Egypt.

Say: Assemble yourselves at Mount Samaria
And see the great terror inside it, and the oppression
    in its midst.

They do not know how to do right—Oracle of
    Yahweh—
Those who store up violence and destruction in their
    royal fortifications.

Therefore this is what the Lord Yahweh said:

An adversary will surround the land
And will bring down your defenses from you,
And your royal fortifications will be plundered.

Verse 9 summons the court, with expert witnesses brought in to condemn Israel, experts who themselves are well known for their violence and cruel inhumanity. Israel's evil is entered as evidence both in verse 9 ("great terror," "oppression") and verse 10 ("violence," "destruction"). Speaking directly to the defendant, Israel, in verse 11 the Lord pronounces the judgment sentence, introduced by "therefore" (Heb. *lākēn*). Israel's judgment sentence is that it will be conquered by a foreign power in a conquest so total that even her best-defended properties—the royal fortifications of Samaria—will be plundered.

Many times, the Prophet Amos does not provide the full covenant lawsuit form but one or two of its elements. Most typically, these are (1) the evidence of covenant breaking and (2) the judgment sentence. Citations of evidence followed by quotations of the Lord's coming judgment are in fact found throughout the book. The key term "therefore" often signals to the reader that the judgment sentence portion of the form is about to begin, although no single verbal clue occurs in every instance. Sometimes other vocabulary associated with court procedure will be an unmistakable indication that the covenant lawsuit concept stands in the background of a given prophetic oracle (e.g., "testify" in 3:13).

Many words of judgment against Israel are recorded in Amos. Most are not given within the framework of the full literary form that we call the covenant lawsuit. All, however, are given on the basis of the Mosaic covenant, in which the Lord promised to punish Israel's sins, in his role as the divine prosecutor of violators of his covenant.

Exile

Jeremiah and Ezekiel are especially known among the prophetical books for their frequent references to the exile of God's people. They both lived at the time of the beginning of the great Babylonian exile of Judah, and it would be surprising if God had not revealed much to them about the significance of that turning point in their nation's history.

Amos, on the other hand, prophesied much earlier (about 760 B.C.), at a time when the nation of (northern) Israel was more prosperous, stronger militarily, and larger geographically than it had been for centuries. Under Jeroboam II (793–753 B.C.), by reason of the mercy of God to the nevertheless wicked nation, Israel had won back territories lost since the days of Solomon (2 Kgs 14:25–28) and was riding the crest of prestige in the international community. It was hardly a time that people would consider the possibility that Israel might be exiled to a foreign land—unless, that is, they were listening to God's prophet, Amos.

It's not that people in 760 B.C. didn't understand what exile was. The deportation of captured populations after warfare had been practiced since at least the beginning of the second millennium (i.e., 2000 B.C.) in the ancient Near East, judging from the three references to it in the epilog of the Babylonian Law of Hammurabi (1728 B.C.). Hittite treaties from the fourteenth and thirteenth centuries B.C. also make reference to the practice of exile. But who would expect exile at a time of national prosperity and power, especially if they didn't take seriously the notion that their nation had offended their national God?

Amos's predictions of Israel's exile were thus not at all well received. They were, in fact, interpreted as a conspiracy to discredit the king (7:10). Proportionately, Amos preached about exile more than any other prophet, and it is little wonder that his frequent words on the subject met with resistance. In Amos, exile is a major theme. In fact, he even preached about the coming exile of nations other than Israel, such as the Arameans (1:5) and the Ammonites (1:15). These words might have seemed welcome to some, if he had not so frequently also announced in the name of the Lord Israel's own coming deportation.

In 5:5–6, Amos attacks the covenantally illegal (Deut 12:2–14) but widespread practice of worshiping at a variety of shrines. The punishments to be expected will include exile:

Don't seek Bethel;
Don't go to Gilgal;
Don't travel to Beersheba!
Because Gilgal will surely go into exile,
And Bethel will become trouble.

Seek Yahweh and live,
Lest he progress like a fire against the family of Joseph
And consume Bethel, with no one to quench it.

This highly patterned poem about three of the favorite
worship centers of the North, all improper rivals of Jerusalem,
mentions three cities, then two cities, then one city, Bethel,
the one place where Amos is known to have preached (7:10-
17). In the mention of Gilgal, the Hebrew wording is allitera-
tive: *gilgal gālōh yigleh*, the words for exile (*gālōh* and *yigleh*)
having prominent *g* and *l* sounds as also found twice in the
name Gilgal (*gilgal*). The point of this clever alliteration was
not for entertainment's sake, however, but a stern warning:
Israel was headed for what in the ancient world was considered a disastrous fate—exile.

Through Amos, God warned Israel even of the geographical destination of their exile. It would be Mesopotamia, according to 5:27, which says "I will exile you past Damascus
said Yahweh, whose name is the God of the Armies." Because
of the configuration of the Fertile Crescent around the great
Arabian Desert, to go east Israelites had first to go north (past
Damascus). The Assyrians in Amos's day were very weak, no
threat to Israel.[6] God, however, was nevertheless planning the
future of his people and of the Assyrians, and, in contrast to
the popular thinking, it was clear from God's revelation that
Israel was headed to Mesopotamian exile.

Amos preached that Israel as a whole would be exiled
(7:11) and made it clear that the prominent people of the

land would not be excepted (6:7; 7:17). He also preached that exile would not be merely a displacement, but an awful ordeal as part of the national destruction:

> If they go into exile in front of their enemies,
> I will command the sword to slay them there.
>
> I will fix my gaze upon them
> For harm and not for benefit. (9:4)

It should be noted that the word "if" does not mean that Israel might escape exile, but that among the many forms of decimation God would employ against his rebellious people, exile was a leading one. As the broader context (9:1-10) indicates (especially 9:1), all Israel would be affected by divine wrath, which would not be limited for any of the people to merely relocation.

The exile occurred just as God through his prophet had promised (2 Kgs 17:3-41), and Israel was never again an independent state among the community of nations. Instead it was made by the conquering Assyrians a part of their empire (722 B.C.), and then became a part of the Babylonian Empire when Babylon completed its conquest of Assyria (605 B.C.), and then passed to the Persians (540 B.C.), the Greeks (333 B.C.), the Ptolemies (323 B.C.), the Seleucids (200 B.C.), the Romans (63 B.C.), etc.

The exile, however, was not to be the final chapter in Israel's history. In addition to predicting the Exile, Amos was also inspired to predict its end. The book closes with this promise from God (9:14-15):

> I will release my people Israel from captivity,
> And they will rebuild the ruined cities and live in
> them.

They will plant vineyards and drink their wine;
They will make gardens and eat their fruit.

I will plant them in their own land so that they will
never again be uprooted from their land which I have
given them, said Yahweh, your God.

These words began to be fulfilled with the decree of
Cyrus in 539 B.C., which allowed deported peoples to return
to their homelands. The Persians did not agree with the
Assyrians and Babylonians that exile was a good way to
punish captured peoples and prevent local populations from
rebelling against their rule. God thus brought into being an
empire that he used to fulfill the promise of Amos 9:14–15.
Of course, the promise of return from exile was only a part
of the grand scheme of restoration, described in part in
Amos 9:11–15 and many other places in the Pentateuch and
Prophets. It was, however, the harbinger of a new era, a
starting point for a new people. The old Israel had been
banished from the old promised land. The new Israel was to
look to a new citizenship (2 Pet 3:13; cf. Acts 3:21; Rom 4:13)
in a place that a postexilic, rebuilt Israel and Jerusalem could
symbolize (Heb 12:18–24; Rev 21:1–4) but never actually
equal.

The prophet as servant: messenger and intercessor

Amos 3:3–8 contains a series of questions showing natural
linkages between certain kinds of events. For example, verse
3 asks, "Do two people travel together without having met?"
and verse 6 asks, "If a trumpet sounds in a city do not the
people tremble?" The purpose of these questions, the answer
to which in each case is yes, is to prepare the hearer/reader
for two main points made in the passage. The first main point

is that of verse 6b, itself also a question: "If there is disaster in a city, has not Yahweh caused it?" It was important that the Israelites realize that their problems were punishments from their God, not random occurrences or neutral events.

The second main point is contained in verses 7 and 8, which argue for the prophetic obligation to pass on to the people the revelation the prophet had received from God:

Indeed, the Lord Yahweh does not do something unless he reveals his counsel to his servants the prophets.

The lion has roared!
Who is not afraid?

The Lord Yahweh has spoken!
Who will not prophesy?

Amos obviously felt that he had no proper option but to obey the calling of God to prophesy. Jonah, an earlier contemporary of Amos, had tried but failed to disobey God's command for him to prophesy to Nineveh. God had been remarkably merciful to Jonah, by pursuing him and forcing him to complete his assignment, however odious it was to the reluctant prophet. In most other cases, God was not nearly so indulgent. Disobedient prophets might even incur fatal wrath (e.g., 1 Kgs 13; Jer 20:1-6; Hos 4:5; cf. Jer 23). As Amos's words suggest, the prophets were supposed to be the Lord's "servants," or as the Hebrew *'bādîm* may also be translated, "slaves" (cf. Jer 7:25).

Being an obedient servant was not easy for the true prophets. It would have been much easier to be one of the many false prophets, since they simply composed in their minds whatever they thought the people would want to hear (and therefore would pay for, prophets being paid by donations, as clergy have always been; cf. Amos 7:12; Luke 8:3).

The Prophet as Servant

Amos ran into the kind of hostility that other obedient prophets had encountered when they preached the truth in places where it was not welcome (7:10-17). Yet there was no other avenue for him to take—other than disobedience—if he was to fulfill the Lord's word.

As a prophet, Amos was automatically a messenger. All prophets understood themselves as messengers sent from God, expected to reproduce faithfully what he had told them to say to the audience he had provided. In the ancient world, people were used to messengers being sent by someone with a message, arriving in a given place and seeking out their audience, speaking the message just as it had been entrusted to them, and then departing. The messenger would begin the text of the message with words such as "This is what X said" and would end portions of the message with reminders such as "said X" or "message of X." Indeed, the prophets routinely employ just such introductions and reminders in their speeches, making it clear that they regard themselves as messengers repeating what they have been told to say to the audience to whom they have been sent. They are clearly not making up their words or choosing their audiences.

In Amos, for example, one finds "This is what Yahweh said" (Heb. *kōh 'āmar yahweh*) introducing each section of the compound oracle against Israel and her neighbor states in 1:3-2:16 (see 1:3, 6, 9, 11, 13; 2:1, 4, 6). Further, one finds many of the individual sections in this same oracle closed by the words "Yahweh said" (Heb. *'āmar yahweh*) or the words "oracle of Yahweh" (Heb. *n'ºum yahweh*) as in 1:5, 8, 15; 2:3, 11, 16. Chapter 4 of Amos is also notable for its frequent reminders that the prophet is not speaking his own word, but Yahweh's, a fact he repeatedly emphasizes by seven times inserting the phrase "oracle of Yahweh" (*n'ºum yahweh*) in the passage.

Amos, like other prophets, employs a number of other variations of these reminders of his messenger role, such as that found in 6:8 ("The Lord Yahweh has sworn by himself . . .") or the introduction to the judgment prediction in 8:7 ("Yahweh has sworn by Jacob's pride . . ."). These and other variations are helpful ways by which we can recognize what scholars sometimes call the "messenger speeches" in the prophetical books. In other words, "Thus says the Lord" and the many similar expressions employed by the prophets are messenger speech "formulas" that identify for us the fact that an obedient servant (prophet) is saying something as a messenger of God.

From time to time one also observes a prophet functioning in a related but distinct role, that of intercessor. An intercessor is simply one who appeals to God for help on behalf of some person or group. Prophets sometimes did this. Abraham and Moses had interceded with God on behalf of cities and nations (Gen 18; Exod 34), and thus prophetic intercession was hardly a new idea. Rather, the prophets' intercession can be understood as representing a natural adjunct to their role as servants, since a servant in the course of his or her duties might reasonably be expected from time to time to ask a master for something on behalf of the family, or other servants, or the like.

Amos's intercession on behalf of the nation of Israel is found in two brief vision accounts. Of the five vision accounts in the book (found in chapters 7-9), the first two contain visions that never actually came to pass—not because they were not true visions of what Yahweh had planned for the future, but because Yahweh in his grace was willing to relent—"change his mind" as the Hebrew *niḥḥam ʿal* is literally translated—based upon the intercessory plea of his servant Amos.

The first account is found in 7:1-3. Amos reports:

This is what Yahweh showed me. He was forming a swarm of locusts when the late planting was beginning to come up—the late planting after the king's mowing. It seemed as if they would completely devour the earth's vegetation. I said, "Lord Yahweh, forgive! How can Jacob survive? He is so small!" Yahweh changed his mind about this. "It will not happen," Yahweh said.

The prophet saw the future being planned, prayed for mercy, and his request was granted. Locust plagues were unstoppable in ancient times. They represented a great agricultural disaster (Deut 28:38, 42; Exod 10:12-15; Joel 1; Amos 4:9). A natural locust plague would be bad enough. A divinely created, supernatural locust plague of the sort Amos saw could ruin all Israel. Amos, of course, had preached judgment against Israel and expected it. Indeed, in the final three visions in the book he sees national disasters that would take place in the future, and he does not attempt to intercede to prevent them. Here, however, was a threat so severe—a divine superplague—that he appealed to the Lord that it not occur. God graciously accepted his prophet's plea, knowing full well, of course, that he had yet other options for punishing his people in mind.

The second vision account (7:4-6) concerns the possibility of destruction by fire:

This is what Yahweh showed me. He was calling for a rain of fire. It devoured the great deep and would have devoured the fields. I said, "Lord Yahweh, stop! How can Jacob survive? He is so small!" Yahweh changed his mind about this as well. "It will not happen," Yahweh said.

This vision account is similar in structure and vocabulary to the prior one. It concerns a somewhat similar sort of threat, the destruction by fire of all the nation's vegetation. ("Fields," Heb. *ḥeleq*, refers here mainly to the land with planted vegetation on it as opposed to, say, rock formations or barren soil.) Note that in Joel 1, locusts and fire are also used together, although metaphorically, as two ways of describing great agricultural devastation caused by the Lord's wrath. Either locusts or fires can ruin a people, taking away their food (cf. Exod 10 with Judg 15:4-5). Once again, however, the threatened future is discarded when the prophet, still an obedient servant and not insubordinate, appeals for mercy from Yahweh.

In the three subsequent visions, Amos sees a future holding for Israel widespread destruction (7:7-9), large-scale death (8:1-3), exile, and slaughter (9:1 10). He can surely have taken no delight in predicting this sort of doom, but he did not appeal for relief from it. The apparent reason is that such punishments, though severe, were not the total sort of destruction represented by the disasters revealed in the first two visions. Amos, in other words, was not trying to prevent Israel from experiencing the wrath of God or trying to show his influence with the Lord by challenging his plans. He knew that Israel had to be punished. He simply prayed for grace to be shown to the disobedient nation he had been sent to preach to (cf. Matt 6:14; Luke 23:34; Acts 17:30).

A final point of interest that these intercession accounts hold for us is that God really is, as Jonah and others confess of him, "gracious, compassionate, patient . . ." (Jonah 4:2; cf. Exod 34:6; Num 14:18; Pss 86:15; 103:8; 145:8; Nah 1:3; Neh 9:17). Intercession is not a manipulation of God. It is an appeal to his character. An obedient servant can certainly make such appeals, trusting that the Master's responses will be just.

The Prophet as Servant

5 OBADIAH

The future of the nations

Obadiah is the Old Testament's shortest book. It contains only a single prophecy, describing God's judgment on Edom and other nations that had oppressed the Israelites by stealing territory from them when the people of Israel were too weak to do anything about it.

In speaking of the future of nations other than Israel, Obadiah is by no means unique. Indeed, the book is a classic example of the category of prophetic literature called "oracles against foreign nations." There are dozens of such oracles in the prophetical books. In fact, every prophetical book in the Old Testament devotes at least some space to the issue of God's plan for various nations of the world, including but by no means limited to his special people, Israel.[1]

There is a basic underlying assumption to all such oracles. It is this: those who are God's people and those who are not will eventually experience different outcomes. The people of

The Future of the Nations

God will be saved and blessed—saved from whatever difficulties, great or small, they or their generation may have encountered. Those who are not God's people will, however, neither be saved nor blessed. They will either be suppressed or destroyed—suppressed within the time bounds of the history of the present world, and/or destroyed from the point of view of eternity.

It is not the case, however, that God is described by the Bible as one who discriminates arbitrarily with regard to the fate of nations. He chooses between or among nations on a consistent covenantal basis, not on the basis of whim or favoritism. The oracles against foreign nations thus do not imply that only ethnic Israelites could be saved or blessed in Old Testament times.[2] Rather, they reflect the fact that God had established a people who were specially his, and had given opportunity to others to join that people or to support them rather than oppose them. In Old Testament times many from other nations did indeed join with the Israelites, and the Law made provision for incorporating such people into the people of God (e.g., Deut 23:8). Others supported Israel, and were blessed for it (Gen 12:3; cf. Isa 19:23-25). Those who broke his covenant of general decency,[3] however, were not to be blessed, and those who opposed his people were by definition opposing him—and deserved his judgment.

Obadiah reflects this assumption. Edom deserved punishment, not because it didn't know any better (cf. Jonah 4:11) but precisely because it did know better. What the nations mentioned in oracles such as Obadiah are to be judged for is that which they knew to be wrong but did anyway. Taking the territory of others is understood worldwide to be wrong—yet that is what Edom did to Israel. While the Babylonians had the Judeans either in captivity or under siege in Jerusalem (i.e., from 588 onwards), the Edomites simply moved in and took over large tracts of land in southern Judah, abandoned by their Judean owners as they fled for safety from the Babylonians (Obad 11-13). (Edom had capitulated to Babylon earlier and thus was not in the same danger that the Judeans were.) The Edomites also captured and turned over to the Babylonians fleeing Judeans (Obad 14) instead of showing compassion toward their brother nation. As a result, the judgment of God described in Obad 1-9 was announced by Obadiah against Edom, including defeat in war, plundering by the enemy, widespread slaughter of the population, and the permanent end of Edom as a threat to Israel.

We can summarize the future for Edom and nations like her compared to Israel: they must decrease because Israel must increase. If Israel is to be saved and blessed, the nations that would naturally try to prevent that from happening must be suppressed and punished. This is the point of Obad 15-21. Employing the terminology of the Day of the Lord,[4] these verses describe how all the nations of the world will be judged, and specifically how those who have done harm to Israel will have their fortunes reversed. In the same way that they oppressed Israel, Israel will now oppress them (v 15)—a punishment perfectly fitting the crime. They will shrink in influence to nothingness (v 16) and be destroyed (v 18). The Israelites will once again inhabit the lands that were rightly theirs according to the divine plan, but which had fallen into the hands of other nations. These included the western coastal plain, during Obadiah's time in the hands of the Philistines (v 19a); Samaria and Gilead, in the hands of the Syrians and Assyrians (v 19b); Zarephath and adjacent southern Phoenician territory in the hands of the Canaanites (v 20a); and the southern Judean region (Negeb) in the hands of Edom (v 20b). The general principle of this portion of the book is that whatever parts of the promised land were not in the possession of the promised people would revert to them in the coming Day of the Lord.

The Future of the Nations

Edom was a prime offender among Israel's immediate neighbor states during the era of Obadiah, so it accordingly receives significant condemnation in this brief book. In other books, other nations are mentioned more frequently (though Edom is virtually always present among those nations being condemned in groups of oracles against foreign nations). The point is that God will one day rule over all the nations of the earth in fulfillment of the prayers of his saints (cf. Ps 82:8; Matt 6:10; cf. John 12:31). Therefore his people the true Israel—from whatever ethnic stock they may be—will enjoy his eternal benefits (Obad 21).

Mount Zion/Jerusalem

In Deut 12:5, the Israelites are told: "You shall seek the place that Yahweh your God will choose from among all your tribes to put his name there for his dwelling." Though it had not yet been identified by name to the Israelites, that place was Jerusalem, the Jebusite city built on a narrow mountain promontory called Mount Zion in the hilly heartland of Canaan. It was David who completed the conquest of Jerusalem by capturing the walled Jebusite central city of Zion (2 Sam 5:6-10) several centuries after Joshua had defeated the city's Jebusite king (Josh 10:1-27; 12:10), and the Israelites, in the days of the Judges, had taken the unwalled outer city, or what we today would call "greater Jerusalem" (Judg 1:8).

David founded the national palace in Zion (1 Sam 5:11-12), and his son, Solomon, built the temple there (1 Kgs 6). With the temple at the highest point on its mount, Zion was the center of Israel, the place where God had caused his name to dwell as a symbol of his presence with his people (cf. 1 Kgs 8:27-29). As the historical headquarters for the kings, it was also appropriately designated as the symbolic seat of government for the Messiah. As Isaiah says, for example, "In the last days the mountain of Yahweh's temple will be established as the chief among the mountains. It will be raised above the hills and all the nations will stream to it" (Isa 2:2). Ezekiel's symbolic vision of the new Jerusalem also describes the Messiah's territory as that of Jerusalem: "What remains on both sides of the holy portion and the city property will belong to the prince" (Ezek 48:21; "prince" is Ezekiel's term for Messiah).

Not surprisingly, then, Obadiah faithfully reflects this concept that Mount Zion/Jerusalem would be the location of the future government of God over all the world on behalf of his people. Obad 17 promises:

> On Mount Zion will be deliverance. It will be a holy place.
> The family of Jacob will dispossess those who dispossessed them.

Obad 21 likewise looks forward to the day when Zion will be the place of refuge for all God's people, the site from which they will reign forever with the Lord:

> Those who have been rescued will go up to Mount Zion
> to rule over the mountains of Esau
> And to Yahweh will belong the kingdom.

In the Old Testament the three terms "Zion," "Mount Zion," and "Jerusalem" are used relatively interchangeably. Obadiah uses "Jerusalem" once (v 11) and "Mount Zion" twice (vv 17, 21). He does not use the single word "Zion" by itself, but does speak in verse 16 of "my holy mountain," one of many other terms used in the Old Testament to refer to Mount Zion/Jerusalem.

The theme of Mount Zion/Jerusalem as the dwelling place of God and the seat of government in the eschaton is

93   *Mount Zion/Jerusalem*

taken up in the New Testament, so that Jerusalem becomes there a symbol of heaven. The coming of the heavenly Jerusalem to earth functions, then, as a symbol of the victory of God over the evils of the earth. Rev 21:2–3 paints this picture beautifully:

> And I saw the holy city, the new Jerusalem, coming down out of heaven from God, prepared as a bride adorned for her husband. And I heard a loud voice from the throne saying "Look, the dwelling of God is with humanity, and he will dwell with them. They will be his people, and God himself will be with them and be their God."

This section of Revelation goes on to reflect further some of the kinds of characteristics that are attributed to Mount Zion in Obadiah. Jerusalem will be a place of refuge (Rev 21:4, 6; cf. Obad 17), a place where God's people belong (Rev 21:7; cf. Obad 17, 21), and a place from which will emanate the judgment of God that eliminates evil (Rev 21:8; cf. Obad 16–18, 21). All Christians are already citizens of Mount Zion/Jerusalem (Heb 12:22–28). They can thus identify with the ancient promises of God through Obadiah concerning their future home.

6   JONAH

Too narrow a view of God's love

God's command to Jonah recorded in 1:2 made it clear to the prophet that he was being asked to undertake an assignment loathsome to him—preaching the possibility of God's mercy to the people of Nineveh, Assyria's leading city, the headquarters of Israel's most powerful enemy among the nations of the world. Jonah 1:2 is often misleadingly translated in modern English versions, giving the reader the impression that God was asking Jonah to preach against Nineveh because of its "evil." In fact, the verse should be rendered: "Go to the important city, Nineveh, and speak against it for their trouble is of concern to me."[1] It was God's concern for the trouble that Nineveh was experiencing that bothered Jonah. Jonah's theology may not have been perfect, as evidenced by the fact that he hoped to "flee out to sea, away from Yahweh" (1:3), as if Yahweh's divine jurisdiction ended or was limited as soon as one departed from the territory of Israel. (The idea that gods had jurisdiction mainly in those nations where they were worshiped was widespread in the ancient Near East; cf. 2 Kgs 17:27; Ezra 1:3; 7:19.) His imperfect theology, however, did not mean that Jonah was not able to hear the word of God clearly and understand its implications. What he heard the Lord telling him did not please him: Nineveh was in trouble, and God wanted his prophet to go there and preach as a means of helping, not harming, the Assyrians.

Assyria was not a nation easy to love by anyone's standards, and it is not surprising that an Israelite prophet should resist the call to a ministry of compassion in its leading city. Assyria had perfected the art of exile, deporting captured populations on a massive scale from their homelands in order to prevent any resurgence of local opposition to the empire's tyrannical rule in its conquered territories. Assyria had also justly gained the reputation of a brutal conqueror. Woe to the nation that tried to hold out against an Assyrian army! Torture and slaughter would be its fate, as was the case in the Assyrian conquest of Egypt (Nah 3:8–10). Indeed, the Assyrian Empire was famous for its cruelty (Nah 3:19).

But to refuse to preach the possibility of divine mercy to one's enemies, no matter how malicious they may be, is simply too narrow a view of God's love. Jonah was a seasoned prophet with plenty of experience in pro-Israelite, anti-foreigner preaching (2 Kgs 14:25). Those sorts of assignments he presumably didn't mind. He understood—correctly—that the enemies of his people were automatically the enemies of his God. That is, after all, a basic assumption of oracles against foreign nations in the prophetical books.[2] What he did not understand—or want to believe—however, was the fact that God actually loved his (God's) enemies. He should have been able to infer this important truth from the long history of God's mercy to Israel, but his view was too narrow. Like most Israelites, he assumed that God automatically loved Israel because it was his own nation, and that God would never think of Israel as an enemy. It fell to Jonah's contemporaries, Hosea and Amos, to preach to the people that their own nation had become God's enemy (Amos 2:6–16; Hos 1:9; etc.) and that other nations than Israel could bear the Lord's name (Amos 9:12). For Jonah, on the other hand, foreigners deserved only hate, Israel only love.

The Book of Jonah ends with a flashback (4:5–11)[3] to the time when Jonah had completed his preaching in Nineveh and had gone outside the city to wait to see whether or not it would repent, and therefore escape God's wrath. In this situation God teaches Jonah a lesson about divine love for people—even evil people—by means of a plant. Jonah builds himself a shelter, undoubtedly of rocks, since "lumber" as we know it was exceedingly rare and expensive in Mesopotamia, where Nineveh was located. The shelter had no roof, but God miraculously gave it one via a leafy gourd that grew up quickly to cover the top of the structure. Jonah had shade, and was "absolutely delighted" with it (4:6). He quickly learned to care about the plant. Then God sent a worm to attack the plant's root and kill it, so that Jonah's shelter was again roofless. God then provided for Jonah a sweltering day, with a hot desert wind, so that he experienced a sort of heat-stroke, and wanted to die (4:7–8). The loss of the plant was to him grievous indeed.

God pointed out how Jonah's view of God's love was too narrow, because his sense of proportion about the value of things was mistaken. Verses 10–11 tell us:

> Yahweh said, "You are so concerned about the climbing gourd which you did not have to lift a finger to grow, which came up overnight and died overnight. Should not I be concerned about Nineveh, the important city which has in it more than a hundred twenty thousand people who do not know their right hand from their left, as well as a large number of animals?"

Too Narrow a View of God's Love

What the Lord refers to here is an implicit scale of value in living things. This scale exists in all cultures, ancient and modern, and is certainly basic to the Scriptures as well. It may be indicated very simply by the following table:

Human Life   (highest value)
Animal Life   (lower value)
Plant Life   (lowest value)

Jonah loved his plant. It was at the bottom of the value scale, but he cared about it very much. To him it had value, and he missed it very much when it was gone. God uses this affection for a plant to make his point about his love for Nineveh. If Jonah loved a plant, at the lowest value level, shouldn't God love the 120,000 people of Nineveh, at the highest value level—or even the animals of Nineveh, at a lower value level than the people but still more valuable than plants?

In other words, people, no matter how wicked, are still valuable to God. They are intrinsically objects of his love. He has created them worthy of his love (cf. Ps 8:3–8), and he definitely loves them. If Jonah could love a plant, God could certainly love people—any people, even Assyrians. The narrow view of God's love is a dangerous one, because it keeps people from being loved by God's people, and leads to discrimination against people on the sorts of bigoted grounds that have been a shame to societies wherever they have surfaced. The Bible hardly portrays God as a "softy." He will judge and destroy the wicked. But he does not do so arbitrarily or capriciously, and as the Scripture so explicitly states, he would prefer not to have to do so (1 Tim 2:4; 2 Pet 3:9). He prefers repentance to judgment, just as he did in Nineveh, and just as Jonah himself grudgingly acknowledges (Jonah 4:2). He has loved the world, not just one nation or people (John 3:16), and our view of his love must never forget that.

Jonah was not, as far as we learn of him in the book that bears his name, stupid. Nor is there anything to suggest that he was arrogant, thinking himself more important than others. He also does not seem to have been dishonest. He fesses up rather forthrightly when the sailors identify him as the cause of the storm that threatens their lives (Jonah 1:9–12), and after his rather dramatic object lesson (1:15–17) he preaches just what God told him to preach, when he gets to Nineveh. He did, of course, try at first to get out of what was for him a highly objectionable assignment, but the book shows no evidence that he lied about his task either to the sailors or to God or to anyone else.

Nevertheless, there is a sense in which Jonah was hypocritical. The word "hypocritical" is used in a variety of ways in modern English; it has, in effect, developed a rather wide range of meaning. Restrictively, it refers to someone's trying to seem something that he or she is not, that is, being phony or pretentious, especially with regard to attempting to seem piously religious when one is actually not. More broadly, however, "hypocritical" tends to designate something or someone who displays ethical inconsistency, as in a self-interested willingness to do one thing while saying that another is right, or to condemn someone else for things that one is himself or herself doing.

In this latter, broader sense, Jonah was hypocritical. He displayed a hypocrisy about the mercy that he received. Grateful to be blessed by divine mercy himself, he was not at all eager to see God give similar mercy to his enemies. That ethical inconsistency is the sort of thing that is popularly called "hypocrisy."

The Book of Jonah itself is structured in such a way as to highlight Jonah's ethical inconsistency. This structure may be represented as follows:

Ch 1: Jonah disobeys God and admits he deserves to die.

Ch 2: After being rescued from death by the fish, he eloquently thanks God for the mercy he has been shown.

Ch 3: Jonah preaches that disobedient Nineveh deserves to die unless it repents.

Ch 4: After Nineveh repents and is rescued from death, Jonah is resentful of the mercy Nineveh is shown.

It is clear in the book that neither Nineveh nor Jonah deserved to be rescued from death. God in his grace nevertheless rescued both. Jonah was glad for this in his own case, but angry about it in the case of Nineveh.

In the structure of the book, it is the psalm that Jonah prays in chapter 2 that especially calls attention to Jonah's hypocrisy. The psalm is of a category that we call a "thanksgiving psalm." Such psalms were composed to be sung or prayed to God in gratitude after a person or group had been delivered from some sort of misery or danger. These psalms typically have a five-part structure:

Thanksgiving Psalm Structure	*Jonah 2:2–9*
Introduction to the psalm	v 2
Description of past trouble	vv 3–6a
Appeal to God for help	v 7
Reference to rescue by God	v 6a
Vow of praise/testimony	vv 8–9

From the picture of Jonah provided in the book, there is every reason to think and no reason to doubt that Jonah was sincerely grateful to God for his own rescue from his own well-deserved punishment. The psalm serves to reinforce this. Far from interrupting the flow of the narrative, it actually heightens the focus on Jonah's ethical inconsistency, because it partially "stops the action" to record his gratitude to God. Here is an exciting story about a man inside a fish, still alive, but instead of details about how it felt for him to be in that predicament, we are given the text of the psalm that he prayed to God in thanksgiving for being alive. (Obviously, he had realized by the time that he prayed the psalm that the fish represented rescue from death.) A poem in the midst of a narrative always draws attention to itself in some way, and this poem is certainly no exception. By the time the reader has finished chapter 2, it is evident that Jonah has accepted, with an eloquent expression of his indebtedness, the gift of life from a God who had every right to put him to death instead (cf. 1:12). Jonah is indeed grateful.

In terms of gratitude, however, Jonah's final attitude resentment) after preaching at Nineveh (4:1) contrasts markedly with that of the people of the wicked city themselves. They show their gratitude almost immediately (3:5) for the chance given to them to repent by the preaching of this stranger who arrives at their gates. In Assyria at this time it was accepted practice that an official visit to an important city (as Nineveh unquestionably was) should take three days: a first day to arrive and declare the purpose of one's visit, a second day to meet with officials and transact whatever business one had come for, and a third day to be sent off on one's return journey. In Jonah 3:3, Nineveh is accordingly referred to as a city requiring a three-day visit. The grateful responsiveness of the people of Nineveh is shown in the fact that they did not wait for the full three days to pass before taking action. As soon as Jonah began preaching—on the first day of his visit (3:4)—the people believed God, called for a fast, and went into mourning as a means of appealing to God for mercy (3:5). The king himself did likewise (3:6) and went further to make the plea, which had started spontaneously on the popular level, a matter of official state policy (3:7-9).

Here was a city and a king only too willing to receive an opportunity from God to be spared—eagerly responding to a chance for life instead of death. The background to their reasons for doing so includes the nature of the troubles in general facing the Assyrian Empire at this time, and the Assyrian tendency toward what we would call superstition,[4] but the point remains that they were glad to have a chance to be spared, and showed their thankfulness by heartfelt actions of repentance. In the same way that Jonah had been glad for deliverance in chapter 2, they are shown to be glad for deliverance in chapter 3.

In chapter 4, however, it is Jonah who is *not* glad for their deliverance, even though he had been very glad about his own in chapter 2. He could rejoice about his own deliverance and they about theirs, but he could not bring himself to rejoice with or for them. His gratitude stopped when others, for whom he had no love, were blessed, too. This is the kind of inconsistency that popularly is called "hypocrisy."

Jonah had fled from God because he knew that God might be compassionate to those he—Jonah—wished to see receive no compassion (4:2). Jonah was grateful, yet his gratitude was limited to himself, and thus ultimately hypocritical.

Forgiveness

As evidenced by its inclusion in that brief compendium of key Christian doctrines known as the Apostle's Creed, the concept of the "forgiveness of sins" is important to our faith. Without forgiveness, after all, how could anyone gain eternal life?

Forgiveness is a rich biblical concept with both human and divine aspects. While God's forgiveness is neither on the same level or of exactly the same type as human forgiveness, there are analogies between the two. This is highlighted by the wording of the Lord's prayer, in which we pray that God will "forgive us our debts as we forgive our debtors" (Matt 6:12). Interestingly, it is this portion of the prayer that Jesus chooses to comment on especially to his disciples: "For if you forgive people when they sin against you, your heavenly Father will also forgive you. But if you do not forgive people their sins, your Father will not forgive your sins" (Matt 6:14–15). This teaching is "honored in the breach" in the life of Jonah.

When Jesus teaches that if we do not forgive those who sin against us, *our* sins will not be forgiven by God, he does not mean God's ability to forgive depends upon ours, or that humans can manipulate God to forgive them merely by being forgiving of others. Rather Jesus' words must be understood as a reminder that repentance is proved in part by forgiveness. The nonforgiving person is not a true follower of Christ. The nonforgiving prophet, likewise, is not in tune with God's will. Indeed, the linkage of repentance and forgiveness, though widely ignored in this age of "easy-believism" is an essential part of the gospel (cf. Mark 1:4; Luke 5:32; 24:47). Jesus taught that our repentance is shown in part by our readiness to forgive those who sin against us: "If your brother sins, rebuke him, and if he repents, forgive him. If he sins against you seven times in a day and seven times comes back to you and says "I repent" [or "I am sorry"], forgive him" (Luke 17:3–4).

There are two levels of forgiveness, but basically only one kind. The levels are the divine and the human. Forgiveness itself, on either level, may be defined simply as not holding something against someone, that is, withholding retribution or punishment. Divine forgiveness is, however, also more than that. First, it involves the withholding of a much greater magnitude of punishment. Second, the withholding of divine punishment is based upon a prior *transfer* of punishment. God never actually overlooks sin. From the divine point of view, sin is always punished. The divine penalty for all sin was paid by Christ. The penalty was taken from those who deserved it and placed upon the only one who did not.

With regard to forgiveness on the human level, consider a question especially relevant to the story of Jonah. Do human beings have the power to forgive? The answer is yes, they do, but there is an important qualification to this answer. On the one hand, human power to forgive is limited to human relationships with other people. Human beings have no power to forgive sin except as it involves their own attitudes and actions toward people who have wronged them. In other words, human forgiveness is a form of self-control, not control over anyone else's destiny. God's forgiveness, on the other hand, involves control over people's temporal and eternal lives. His power to punish goes far beyond any human power to punish. In the Book of Jonah, God's power to forgive had great consequence. Jonah's did not. God exercised his forgiveness. Jonah withheld his.

The prophets speak fairly often of divine forgiveness, and only rarely of human forgiveness. The Book of Jonah addresses both. Generally in the prophetical books, three Hebrew verbal roots are commonly used in referring to the concept of God's forgiveness of sin: *slḥ*, which has a range of meaning roughly the same as the English word "forgive"; *nśʾ*, which in addition to "forgive" can mean "lift" or "remove"; and *kpr*, which is most often translated "atone." The prophets also convey the concept of forgiveness in images that do not necessarily contain any of these particular vocabulary words. Examples of the latter would include Micah 7:19, ("you will tread our sins underfoot and hurl all our iniquities into the depths of the sea"), Isa 43:25 ("I, even I am he who blots out your transgressions for my own sake and remembers your sins no more"), and Jer 31:34 ("For I will forgive their wickedness and remember their sins no more"). In the case of Jonah, the concept of forgiveness is much more strongly conveyed by the situation described in the story than by the use of vocabulary usually associated with forgiveness.

Most of the time that the prophets speak about forgiveness, it is God's forgiveness of Israel that they refer to, and particularly God's forgiveness of Israel in the "latter days," the eschatological era when he will have created for himself a new people to reflect his glory, a righteous people characterized by the fact that their sins have been forgiven (cf. the passages cited above and, e.g., Isa 33:24; Jer 33:8; Hos 14:2). As Jeremiah quotes God, "I will forgive the remnant that I spare" (Jer 50:20). The new age to come will be delineated in part by the general availability of the forgiveness of sins to all who believe.

This was by no means obvious under the Old Covenant. In fact, it represents one of the advances of the New Covenant over the Old. This is not to say that the means of forgiveness was ultimately different in the Old Covenant, only to say that the fact of righteousness by faith was hardly understood widely or clearly by Old Testament figures in an age which assumed that righteousness was earned by ritual sacrifice and the keeping of a covenant complicated by many stipulations.

There are, however, other emphases in the prophetical books on forgiveness, especially the sort that we might call "temporal." In the story of Jonah, three kinds of temporal forgiveness may be considered as either described or implied:

1. *God's forgiveness of Jonah.* Jonah deserved death but was rescued instead. This was hardly a general forgiveness of Jonah's sins, a topic not in purview in the book. It was a temporal forgiveness of one act of rebellion, that is, Jonah's running from God's assignment to preach at Nineveh.

2. *God's forgiveness of Nineveh.* The city, like Jonah when he was running from God, deserved death and, like Jonah, was rescued instead. This was, likewise, not a permanent forgiveness of all that Assyria had done, but temporal

forgiveness provided to a generation of inhabitants, involving no guarantees for the longer term.

3. *Jonah's forgiveness of Nineveh*. This, of course, is notable by its absence. It didn't occur—but it should have. Jonah even tried to avoid being part of the process whereby God could forgive—even temporally—the Ninevites. He thus implicitly demonstrated that he was unwilling to forgive them himself. He wanted to go on hating his enemies, the Assyrians, and how could he do that while at the same time forgiving them? On the one hand, hating and forgiving are, after all, incompatible. Loving and forgiving, on the other hand, go together.

The relationship of love and forgiveness is an important one. Micah says of God: "Who is a God like you, who pardons sins and forgives the transgression of the remnant of his inheritance? You do not stay angry forever but delight to show mercy" (Mic 7:18). He says these words, of course, about God's mercy to Israel—the true eschatological Israel made up from all peoples and nations. The description is also generally characteristic of God's willingness to forgive, a willingness that in the case of the Book of Jonah was exercised even on behalf of a people as despicable as the Assyrians. This is what Jonah resents having to acknowledge. As the story says,

> This [the sparing of Nineveh] was absolutely disgusting to Jonah and he became angry. He prayed to Yahweh: "This, O Yahweh, is exactly what I said when I was back in my own country. That is why I fled, earlier, on the open sea. I knew that you were a God who is gracious, compassionate, patient, firmly loyal, and one who decides against disaster. So, Yahweh, take my life from me. I would rather be dead than alive" (Jonah 4:1–3).

Being forgiven by God is easy for anyone to take. Who would turn it down? Taking pleasure, however, in seeing God forgive one's enemies—people who really are evil—that is another matter. The first sort of forgiveness was fine with Jonah. The other would have involved loving people so maddening to him that he preferred to die rather than see it happen.

Accordingly, an important question, not expressed in so many words in the book but nevertheless raised for the thoughtful reader by the story of Jonah is: Are we like the reluctant prophet? Do we readily accept the forgiveness God has provided for us in Christ but resist the idea that similar forgiveness should be granted to those who have harmed us? Do we resent some of the forgiving that God does because it is in our minds letting evil people—other evil people—get away with something? That is a question the Book of Jonah leaves with us. It is an important question for us to ask.

NOTES

Chapter 2   Hosea

1. G. Mendenhall, "Covenant Forms in Israelite Tradition." *Biblical Archaeologist* 17 (1954) 50–76; idem, *Law and Covenant in the Ancient Near East* (Pittsburgh: Biblical Colloquium, 1955).

2. E.g., M. G. Kline, *Treaty of the Great King* (Grand Rapids: Eerdmans, 1963).

3. Hos 1; 2; 2:2, 5; 3:3; 4:10, 11, 12, 15, 18; 5:3; 6:10; 9:1. In some verses the term occurs more than once.

4. For a fuller discussion, see WBC 31:70, 72, 76.

5. Because the consonantal (original) Hebrew spelling of "in miseries" and "in boats" is identical, many modern versions incorrectly choose "in boats" as part of the translation of Deut 28:68.

6. See WBC 31:xxxi–xlii.

7. Heb. literally "and I also to you," thus RSV "so will I also be to you" [i.e., having no relations]. NIV "and I will live with you" is exactly the opposite of what the Heb. intends.

8. E.g., Krister Stendahl, "The Apostle Paul and the Introspective Conscience of the West," *Harvard Theological Review* 56 (1963): 199–215; also in S. E. Miller and G. E. Wright, eds., *Ecumenical Dialogue at Harvard: The Roman Catholic-Protestant Colloquium* (Cambridge, Mass.: Belknap Press Fund of Harvard University

Press, 1964), 236-56; cf. Karl Menninger, *Whatever Became of Sin?* (New York: Hawthorne Books, 1973).

9. Ze'ev Meshel, "Did Yahweh Have a Consort?" *Biblical Archaeology Review* 5:2 (1979): 24-35.

10. See WBC 31:171-72.

Chapter 3 Joel

1. For the evidence, see Douglas Stuart, "The Sovereign's Day of Conquest," *Bulletin of the American Schools of Oriental Research* 221 (1976): 159-64.

2. E.g., Jer 20:7-18.

3. See esp. WBC 31:xxxiv-xxxvii.

4. See above, The Distant Past and the Ultimate Future: The Long View on Israel.

Chapter 4 Amos

1. On these contrasts see above ch 2, The Attractions of Idolatry.

2. See above, ch 2, The Distant Past and the Ultimate Future: The Long View on Israel.

3. See above, ch 2, The Reliance of the Prophets on the Law.

4. See R. deVaux, *Ancient Israel* (New York: McGraw-Hill, 1965), 113-14.

5. For fuller documentation on the covenant lawsuit, see J. Harvey, "Le Rîb-pattern." *Biblica* 43 (1962): 172-96; H. B. Huffmon, "The Covenant Lawsuit in the Prophets," *Journal of Biblical Literature* 78 (1959): 285-95; L. A. Sinclair, "The Courtroom Motif in the Book of Amos." *Journal of Biblical Literature* 85 (1966): 351-355; G. E. Wright, "The Lawsuit of God," in B. W. Anderson and W. Harrelson, eds., *Israel's Prophetic Heritage* (New York: Harper and Row, 1962), 62-67.

6. See WBC 31:440-42, 490-92

Chapter 5 Obadiah

1. For a complete listing, see WBC 31:405-6.

2. In this regard, it is useful to note that the nation of Israel

was never ethnically pure (as evidenced in Exod 12:38; Josh 6:25; Judg 1:16; Ruth 4:18-22; etc.).

3. See above, ch 4, Yahweh's Universal Sovereignty.

4. See above, ch 3, The Day of the Lord.

Chapter 6 Jonah

1. The Heb. word *rā'ah* often means "trouble" rather than "evil." Cf. WBC 31:444, 447-50. On the nature of Nineveh's troubles in Jonah's day, see 31:440, 490-92.

2. See above, ch 5, The Future of the Nations.

3. On the identification of Jonah 4:5-11 as a flashback, see WBC 31:499-501.

4. WBC 31:490-94.

BIBLIOGRAPHY

Allen, L. C. *The Books of Joel, Obadiah, Jonah and Micah.* New International Commentary on the Old Testament. Grand Rapids, Mich.: Eerdmans, 1976.

Bartlett, J. "The Brotherhood of Edom." *Journal for the Study of the Old Testament* 2 (1977): 2-27.

Bright, J. *Covenant and Promise: The Prophetic Understanding of the Covenant in Pre-Exilic Israel.* Philadelphia: Westminster Press, 1975.

Craigie, P. *Twelve Prophets.* Vol 1. Daily Bible Study Series. Philadelphia: Westminster Press, 1984.

Gemser, B. "The Rîb or Controversy Pattern in Hebrew Mentality." *Vetus Testamentum Supplements* 3 (1955): 124-37.

Gordon, C. H. "The Wine-Dark Sea." *Journal of Near Eastern Studies* 37 (1978): 51-52.

Harrison, R. K. *Introduction to the Old Testament.* Grand Rapids, Mich.: Eerdmans, 1969.

Hayes, J. H. "The Usage of Oracles against Foreign Nations in Ancient Israel." *Journal of Biblical Literature* 87 (1968): 81-92.

Hillers, D. *Treaty-Curses and the Old Testament Prophets.* BibOr 16. Rome: Pontifical Biblical Institute, 1964.

Hubbard, D. *With Bands of Love: Lessons from the Book of Hosea.* Grand Rapids, Mich.: Eerdmans, 1969.

Huffmon, H. "Prophecy in the Mari Letters." *Biblical Archaeologist* 31 (1968): 101–24.

———. "The Covenant Lawsuit in the Prophets." *Journal of Biblical Literature* 78 (1959): 285–95.

Kaiser, W. "The Promise of God and the Outpouring of the Holy Spirit: Joel 2:28–32 and Acts 2:16–21." In *The Living and Active Word of God: Essays in Honor of Samuel J. Schultz.* Edited by M. Inch and R. Youngblood. Winona Lake, Ind.: Eisenbrauns, 1983.

Keil, C. F. *The Twelve Minor Prophets.* Biblical Commentary on the Old Testament. Grand Rapids, Mich.: Eerdmans, 1969.

Landes, G. M. "The Kerygma of the Book of Jonah." *Interpretation* 21 (1967): 3–31.

Mays, J. L. *Amos: A Commentary.* Old Testament Library. Philadelphia: Westminster Press, 1969.

———. *Hosea.* Old Testament Library. Philadelphia: Westminster Press, 1969.

Mendenhall, G. *Law and Covenant in the Ancient Near East.* Pittsburgh: Biblical Colloquium, 1955.

Meyers, J. "Edom and Judah in the Sixth-Fifth Centuries B. C." In *Near Eastern Studies in Honor of William Foxwell Albright,* edited by H. Goedicke, 377–92. Baltimore: Johns Hopkins Press, 1971.

Moran, W. L. "New Evidence from Mari on the History of Prophecy." *Biblica* 50 (1969): 15–56.

Motyer, J. A. *The Day of the Lion.* Downers Grove, Ill.: InterVarsity Press, 1974.

Payne, D. "Jonah from the Perspective of Its Audience." *Journal for the Study of the Old Testament* 13 (1979): 3–12.

Stuart, D. *Hosea-Jonah.* Word Biblical Commentary 31. Waco, Tex.: Word Books, 1987.

———. "The Old Testament Prophets' Self-Understanding of Their Prophecy." *Themelios* (1980/81): 9–14.

Watts, J. D. W. "An Old Hymn Preserved in the Book of Amos." *Journal of Near Eastern Studies* 15 (1956): 33–39.

————. *The Books of Joel, Obadiah, Jonah, Nahum, Habakkuk, and Zephaniah.* Cambridge Bible Commentary. Cambridge: Cambridge University Press, 1975.

Wiseman, D. "Jonah's Nineveh." *Tyndale Bulletin* 30 (1979): 29–51.

Reference	Page	Reference	Page	Reference	Page
28:68	26, 109	17:27	96	33:8	105
30	29	23:6	37	50:20	105
30:4-5	27	23:7	18		
		25:9	12	**Ezekiel**	
Joshua				8:9	17
6:25	111	**2 Chronicles**		13:5	47
7	42	20:15	54	16	38
10:1-27	92			18	33
12:10	92	**Ezra**		19	50
		1	43	27	50
Judges		1:3	96	30	50
1:8	92	7:19	96	33:1-20	33
1:16	10, 111			39:29	60
3:7	37	**Nehemiah**		48:21	93
5:20	53	9:17	87		
9:45	52			**Hosea**	
15:4-5	52, 87	**Psalms**		1-3	38
19	42	8:3-8	98	1:2	2, 21, 22, 28, 34, 109
		14:6	66	1:4	42
Ruth		45	38	1:4-5	28
4:18-22	111	82:8	92	1:5	27
		86:15	87	1:6	28
1 Samuel		103:8	87	1:7	54
5:11-12	92	140:12	66	1:9	3, 27, 28, 31, 97
8	42	145:8	87	1:10-11	43
17:36	53			1:10-2:1	28
		Isaiah		1:11	31
2 Samuel		2:2	93	2:1	31
1:19-27	50	11:4	66	2:2	38, 109
5:6-10	92	13:6	47	2:2-15	34, 38
		13:9	47	2:2-20	2
1 Kings		14:4-23	50	2:3	28
6	92	19:23-25	90	2:4-5	28
8:27-29	92	25:4	66	2:5	38, 109
12:28-33	14	32:15	60	2:6	28
13	83	33:24	105	2:7	23, 38
18:18	64	42:13	54	2:8	12
18:19	37	43:25	104	2:9-13	28
19:18	18	44:3	60	2:10	38
19:21	5	54:6	38	2:12	38
		63:10-11	59	2:13	23, 28, 38
2 Kings				2:14	38
3:19	52	**Jeremiah**		2:14-23	28
3:25	52	3:1	38	2:15	41, 42
6:1-2	5	7:25	83	2:16-23	13, 43
14:25	7, 96	20:1-6	83	2:18	13
14:25-28	79	20:7-18	110	2:23	31
15:8-12	73	23	83	3	32
17:3-41	80	31:34	56, 104	3:1-5	2

Index of Scriptures

Reference	Page	Reference	Page	Reference	Page
3:14	3, 4, 46, 47, 49	3:11	74	9:7	65
3:15–16	58	3:13	64, 78	9:10	66
3:16	59	3:15	75	9:11–13	66
3:17	59	4	84	9:11–15	66, 82
3:17–21	50	4:1	5, 69, 74	9:12	5, 65, 97
3:18	59	4:6–8	66	9:14–15	81, 82
3:19	59	4:6–11	30		
3:19–21	57	4:9	66, 86	**Obadiah**	
3:20	57, 59	4:10	66	1–9	91
3:21	59	4:13	64	11	93
4:1–21	55	5	47	13	6
4:2	62	5:5–6	79	14	6, 91
4:9	62	5:7	5	15–21	91
4:9–11	55	5:8	64	16	93
4:9–16	55	5:11	75	16–18	94
4:12	62	5:11–12	69	17	93, 94
4:16	55	5:12	75	17–21	6
		5:17	51	21	92, 93, 94
Amos		5:18–27	47		
1	5	5:21–24	5, 18	**Jonah**	
1:2	66	5:27	80	1	100
1:3–5	65	6:1	5	1:1	7
1:3–2:3	68	6:1–7	5, 74, 75	1:2	95
1:3–2:16	84	6:7	81	1:3	95
1:4	12	6:8	85	1:3ff.	7
1:5	79	7–9	85	1:9–12	99
1:6–7	65	7:1	66	1:12	101
1:7	12	7:1–3	85, 86	1:15–17	99
1:9–10	65	7:4–6	86	2	100, 101, 102
1:10	12	7:7–9	87	2:1–10	7
1:11–12	65	7:9	72	2:2–9	100, 101
1:13–15	65	7:10	79	2:8	14
1:15	79	7:10–13	5	3	100, 102
2	5	7:10–17	72, 80, 84	3:2	7
2:1–3	65	7:11	66, 80	3:4	101
2:2	12	7:12	73, 83	3:5	101
2:4–5	68	7:13	73	3:5–9	7
2:5	12	7:14	73	3:6	101
2:6–7	67	7:14–15	5	3:7–9	101
2:6–8	5	7:16–17	73, 74	4	100, 102
2:6–16	68, 97	7:17	66, 81	4:1	101
2:7	18	8:1–3	87	4:1–3	7, 106
2:8	18, 67	8:4–6	70, 71	4:2	87, 98, 102
2:12	73	8:5–6	5	4:5–9	7
2:13–16	69	8:7	71, 85	4:5–11	97, 98, 111
3:1	5	9:1–10	81, 87	4:11	90
3:1–2	75, 76, 77	9:2–4	66		
3:3–8	82, 83	9:4	81	**Micah**	
3:9–11	77, 78	9:5	66	7:18	106
3:10	74	9:5–6	64, 65	7:19	104

Index of Scriptures